v6

Everything You Need to Know about IPv6 to Save Your Job, Save Your Sanity, and Make More Money

RICHARD KULLMANN

Kullmann Publishers

Published by Kullmann Publishers

Copyright © 2017 by Richard Kullmann

Kullmann Publishers
428 East Thunderbird Road #746
Phoenix, AZ 85022
E-mail: KullmannPublishers@gmail.com

Publishing and editorial team: Author Bridge Media, www.AuthorBridgeMedia.com
Project Manager and Editorial Director: Helen Chang
Editor: Katherine MacKenett
Publishing Manager: Laurie Aranda
Publishing Assistant: Iris Sasing
Cover design: Mark Gelotte
Interior illustrations: Richard Kullmann

Library of Congress Control Number: 2017906058
ISBN: 978-0-9988750-1-9 -- paperback
978-0-9988750-2-6 -- hardcover
978-0-9988750-0-2 -- ebook
978-0-9988750-3-3 -- audiobook

Ordering Information:

Quantity sales. Special discounts are available on quantity purchases by corporations, associations, and others. For details, contact the publisher at the address above.

Printed in the United States of America

DEDICATION

If it were not for one person in particular, this book never would have happened. Regretfully, he is now with us only in spirit. I dedicate this book to the man, the myth, the legend, the one and only Tim Sweeney.

CONTENTS

ACKNOWLEDGMENTS

Writing a book can be tough, and fully completing it can seem like an impossible task at times. Be it for moral support, guidance, a kick in the ass, or even showing me a cool new way to cut and eat a delicious home-grown grapefruit, many people have pushed me along through this process.

I would like to thank Helen Chang, Katherine MacKenett, and the rest of the Author Bridge Media team for the guidance they have provided me throughout this process (and for putting up with me through it all). I would also like to thank my family and friends, who have been with me every step of the way.

WHY BUY, OR STEAL, THIS BOOK: AN INTRODUCTION BY THE AUTHOR

> *"Hello, you have reached the IT department. Have you tried turning it off and back on again?"*

What's the Problem?

You picked up this book for a reason.

It could be that you are simply trying to gain, or maintain, a technology certification. Most networking certifications now include elements of IPv6. Perhaps you are an engineer and have been told that you have to migrate the network. Maybe you are a CIO and need to gain a better understanding of the technology so that you can explain it better to the board, or so you will better understand what your engineers are trying to tell you. Maybe it was just because this book was closest to the door of the store and made for an easy exit with it stuffed inside your jacket.

You knew IPv6 was coming, but who wants to take on a new project that touches practically every element in your network? If you do it wrong, the new multimillion-dollar video conferencing system you just deployed company-wide may stop working. You may open up security holes in your network. The CEO may miss some emails or, worse, not be able to reach his favorite porn site.

Life is stressful enough with the endless stream of new technologies to deploy and keep up with, just so you can replace them with something else in the next year or two. Unless you're the government, most people want to prioritize their task list based on the "if it's not broke, don't fix it" concept.

That is no longer a good enough approach for IP.

In 2011, the Internet Assigned Numbers Authority held a ceremony and allocated its final five IPv4 prefixes, exhausting its pool of IPv4 addresses. In 2015, the American Registry of Internet Numbers depleted its pool of IPv4 addresses. Although service providers began stockpiling IPv4 address space in the mid-2000s to expand the lifetime of IPv4, now it is no longer a question of if you are going to migrate to IPv6.

It is a question of when you will be forced to.

How Can We Make It Better?

So how can you fix all of this?

You can retire from the technology-related work and become an aspiring musician/barista, or you can learn how IPv6 works.

Once you really understand how IPv6 works, you will see that it is easier to work with than IPv4. Even though the address format looks much more complicated, it is very streamlined and simplified. Many of the behaviors of IPv6 are based on years of hindsight from working with IPv4 and were designed to make it more efficient. Not only does it allow for a virtually endless number of addresses, but it streamlines the process, making it easier for anyone to work with.

As you go through this book, you should feel any stress you

have about IPv6 melt away. Addressing will make more sense. All of your current systems will continue to work, during and after the migration. The CEO will still be able to email and surf, and the network will stay as secure as it was to begin with.

As for the technology certifications, you will probably understand IPv6 better than whoever wrote the test questions. (True story.)

Who Am I?

How do I know all of this?

From the time I first started working with technology, be it building personal computers or building networks, it has always been a trial by fire. I basically learned the technology by jumping in and figuring it out very quickly.

Really, there was a fire inside a computer.

Did you know that you can actually attach the D-shaped power connector to a hard disk drive backwards? I didn't know you could until a student in a Service & Support class I was teaching managed to do it. The student called me over to help troubleshoot why the computer would not boot up and why a funny smell was coming from inside the case. When we opened the case, chips on the hard disk were still bubbling. That was in the mid-1990s.

IPv6 was no different for me. How did I learn about it? The way I have tried to learn about most technologies is to jump in and tear them apart to see what they were doing. I would connect a sniffer to the network so I could capture and decode each packet to see what was happening as I configured the systems.

Using more than twenty years of experience working with and teaching IPv6, I have tried to make it much easier for you to learn.

I have been a consultant and technology instructor since the late 1980s in computer systems, networking technologies, and security. I've been a Certified Novell Instructor (CNI), Microsoft Certified Trainer (MCT), and Cisco Certified Systems Instructor (CCSI), as well as an instructor for McAfee, Network Associates, Entercept Security Technologies, Intruvert Networks, and Ciena. I developed several training programs and created the Intrusion Prevention System program for Network Associates (now McAfee again).

I began working with IPv6 in 1996 when networks started migrating from Novell to Microsoft, and therefore from IPX to IPv4, at a rapid pace. We started using up the IPv4 address space very quickly, and because I could see the need for it, I wanted to be ready for the change.

Since then, I have taught scores of weeklong classes on IPv6 and have helped thousands of people learn about it. I have also provided subject matter expert services to many organizations globally, from small businesses to international organizations.

But this is not about me. It's about you. So how do you get started learning all of this?

How to Read This Book

This book is organized so that if you are starting with absolutely no knowledge of IPv6, each chapter will prepare you for the next. If you are familiar with elements of it, or if you don't care about parts of it such as the history or routing, you can certainly pick any chapter that you want to read and should still get the point.

Feel free to jump around as necessary and look at what you are most interested in. For example, if you understand how binary, decimal, and hexadecimal work, then you do not need to read the chapter on the math. You must understand binary to hexadecimal to understand the IPv6 address, though, so the section is there if you need it.

We do not get into specific commands used to configure IPv6 in here. There are too many different vendors and operating systems for me to be able to fully cover all the configurations. At the end of the book, I'll show you where you can get more configuration-specific information.

Let's Rock

I have felt the overwhelming stress of having to learn, become an expert on, and deploy new technologies on a deadline. Stick with me through this, and you'll be looking back on it saying, "That wasn't so hard."

I wrote this book to help you understand the essential behavior of IPv6. We will start out with a basic understanding of where IPv6 came from and then take a step-by-step approach to break it down so that you will fully understand how it works. When you finish this book, you will have a firm understanding of how IPv6 operates.

Now, let's rock.

Chapter 1

In the Beginning: A Brief History of the Internet Protocol

What was the first message ever transmitted across the "internet"?

Answer: lo (It was supposed to be "login," but the system crashed after the "lo.")

In the Beginning . . .

It is the cool, foggy, Monday morning of October 9, 1967. A two-day meeting is about to start, led by a Pentagon official named Bob Taylor. This meeting, unknown to anyone attending, is about to forever change the future of the world.

A division of the Pentagon known as the Advanced Research Projects Agency (ARPA) is going to start a project to connect computer systems in multiple locations. The purpose of this is to allow different facilities to share the computer resources.

This project network is what became known as the "ARPANET."

The ARPANET turned out to be so successful that it later evolved into what is now known as the internet, and it has caused pleasure for millions of people . . . and pain for many network engineers, ever since.

Fast forward a few decades, and now almost everything you touch is, in some way, connected to the network that started from that small meeting. It is no longer just a network of computer systems but is now considered a much broader "Internet of Things" (IoT) or even the "Internet of Everything."

Which takes us to IPv6.

What Is Internet Protocol Version 6 (IPv6)?

In the shortest, simplest answer to the question "What is IPv6?" I would have to say it is a really, really big address. At a basic level, THAT IS IT. Did I mention it's big? Okay, if you just want to know at a basic level what IPv6 is, you can stop reading now. Thank you for your time and for buying this book. Goodbye.

If you want to know more, keep reading.

You're still here? Cool, let's continue then.

IPv6 was developed as an enhancement (version 6) of the Internet Protocol. The primary purpose was to allow many more device addresses than were previously available, but it also includes many features to make it more user friendly. This allows for a more streamlined approach to device deployment.

Today we have many more types of devices connecting to the network than in the past. Back in the 1990s, for example, telephones had their own separate network, known as the Public Switched Telephone Network (PSTN), but today most phones are communicating by Voice over Internet Protocol (VoIP). Cameras, security device readers, even appliances are connecting to the IP network. IPv6 allows for this continuing evolution.

Several organizations have exhausted their entire assigned IPv4 address space, including all of the private address space, and still do not have enough addresses for all the devices they need to enable. They had no choice but to migrate to IPv6. Just think about all of the "smart meters" being deployed to every house, apartment, condo, office, and billboard, for instance. There are a lot of devices that need addresses.

To really grasp all of this, you should understand where the internet came from.

Let's Start with a Little Basic Background

The ARPANET was designed based on the concept of packet switching, a method developed by Paul Baran for the RAND Corporation. The basis for a packet-switching network was to create a network that could survive a nuclear attack.

Packet switching is a store-and-forward operation. The originating device, known as a "host," generates a grouping of information to transmit, called a packet, and forwards the packet to its first intermediate forwarding device, such as a switch or router. Each intermediate device will forward the packet to the next device based on destination address information contained within the packet. This process continues until the packet reaches its final destination host.

This is very similar to the forwarding of a letter through the intermediate post offices from the sender to the receiver. In fact, in the original specification, the term "letter" was used to refer to the packet, and the term "post office" was used to refer to the routers.

The Internet Transmission Control Program (TCP)

Okay, IT people, right now you are probably thinking, "What an idiot; he doesn't know what 'TCP' stands for." I did not call it the wrong name. Just follow along and I will explain.

When ARPA started trying to connect multiple computer systems in remote locations together, many issues came up. How do you address the devices for reachability? How do you make sure the packets arrive at their destinations intact? How do you control the communication flows?

In 1974, a "request for comments" (RFC) was published defining an Internet Transmission Control Program, called "TCP."

TCP defined how to encapsulate the data being transmitted as a way to control the communication process. In the original form, the TCP protocol covered both the layer 3 and the layer 4 operations of what we know today as the Open System Interconnection (OSI) reference model.

In 1978, TCP was split into the two different protocols we use today, TCP (renamed to Transmission Control Protocol) and Internet Protocol (IP).

Note: The Open System Interconnection (OSI) model is a seven-layer model that was defined by the International Standards Organization (ISO) in 1984. Its purpose is to simplify the operations and understanding of data communications. Even though TCP was created a decade earlier, and based on its own layered model, we always refer to protocol positions in the stack in relation to the OSI model. It's that whole "standards" thing.

The IP version 4 address consists of 32 bits, divided into four 8-bit groupings, called "octets." Each octet is represented by its decimal value and separated from each other octet by a period.

IPv4 example: 172.16.4.37

A portion of the 32-bit address is used to identify the "network number." This portion identifies the network that a host is attached to, similar to the street name in a house mailing address. The rest of the 32-bit address identifies the "local address" and is used to identify the individual host on the network, similar to the individual house on the street. The size of each portion of the address is identified by using a subnet mask.

How Is v6 Better?

IP version 6 (IPv6) was defined in 1995 (and further updated in 1998) to address some limitations and considerations with IPv4. Specifically, five issues were addressed:

- Larger address space
- A simplified header format
- Improved extensions and options
- Flow labeling
- Authentication and privacy

In IPv4, you have only 32 bits for addressing, so that gives you a grand total of only 4,294,967,296 combinations. Yes,

I said "only." According to the United Nations Department of Economic and Social Affairs, there were approximately 7.4 billion people on the earth as of June 2016. So assuming everyone needed one address, we would not be close to having enough.

Now, add to this the fact that we cannot even use all the 32-bit address space.

There are 571,539,456 addresses from those 32 bits that are unassignable for public internet use just because of classification and other reservations. That leaves us about half the address space we would need just to assign every person in the world a single address.

Here is the breakdown.

Total addresses	4,294,967,296
Loopback (127.x.x.x)	(−16,777,216)
Private "Class A"	(−16,777,216)
Private "Class B"	(−1,048,576)
Private "Class C"	(−65,536)
Multicast	(−268,435,456)
Experimental/Other	(−268,435,456)
Usable addresses	3,723,427,840

Compound that by the fact that many people have more than one address they are using. Today, a typical "connected" person uses at least three devices with IP addresses at a time. This may be your desk phone using Voice over IP (VoIP), your computer, and your mobile phone, as an example.

IPv6's Larger Address Space

IPv6 uses 128 bits instead of IPv4's 32 bits.

Because we are talking in binary combinations (binary is further explained in the next chapter), each bit you add doubles the number of combinations you can get. To calculate the total number of combinations, you use the formula 2^n = total combinations (n = number of bits).

For example:

2^1 = 2 combinations from 1 bit   (0, 1)
2^2 = 4 combinations from 2 bits   (00, 01, 10, 11)
2^3 = 8 combinations from 3 bits   (000, 001, 010, 011
                                            100, 101, 110, 111)

Fig 1.1

So, adding 1 more bit will double the total combinations you can get from just two bit values (0 or 1). If we expanded the address space from 32 bits to just 33 bits, that would double the address space from 4,294,967,296 to 8,589,934,592 possible addresses.

Did I mention that IPv6 addresses are really big?

IPv6 expands the address space to 128 bits, four times the size of IPv4. Now if you want to know what that comes out to, here it is:

2^{128} = 340,282,366,920,938,463,463,374,607,431,768,211,456

Fig 1.2

Who wants to try to say that number? I'll give you a hint: it starts with 340 undecillion.

With the IPv6 address space, we no longer have the issue of not having enough available addresses for . . . pretty much anything. Just like in IPv4, there are large blocks of address space that are unusable for public assignment, but there is still a huge number of addresses available for use.

Okay, so you get a big address. What about the simplified header? What about the improved extensions and options support? What is flow labeling, and what are the authentication and privacy capabilities?

I'm getting to all of that; keep reading.

The Path to IPv6 Enlightenment

Even though you can simply jump to any chapter you have the most interest in, I have systematically arranged this book so that you can start with very little knowledge of IP and build on it chapter by chapter.

Math time. You need to understand how hexadecimal works in order to fully understand how IPv6 addressing works. We will review the basics of binary, conversion to decimal, and conversion to hexadecimal to establish that base understanding.

Now that's scary looking: To make the 128-bit address space user friendly, an easy way to represent the address had to be established. We will examine the representation rules in detail.

We're going global, baby. To understand what an address means, you have to know what the different elements of the address are. We will look at each part of the address and how it gets assigned.

We're gonna need a bigger box. To be able to transport packets with this large address, the IP encapsulation header had to be modified. We will examine this header format as well as the use of extension header encapsulations.

Your host has control issues. To manage communications, IPv6 relies on control messages between devices. We will look at how IPv6 uses the Internet Control Message Protocol (ICMP) in several ways to be able to operate correctly.

Get your kicks, on route IPv6. You cannot communicate with anyone who is not on your directly connected network without proper routing. Routers must be able to build and maintain tables in order to forward packets. We will look at common protocols to support this and see why you may choose one over another.

Watch out for the worms. If you have a hybrid network with areas that transport only IPv4 traffic, you must have a transition methodology. We will look at "dual stack" implementation as well as different tunneling methods.

IPv4? We Don't Need No Stinking IPv4. If you do not have a strategic plan for migrating protocols, you could run into a lot of problems. Although no two networks are exactly the same, there are some similar considerations when starting a migration to IPv6. I will show you a common path that I use to manage migrations.

I know this can look very overwhelming. Not only do you have that long, funny-looking address to deal with, but we have all these other considerations as well. Don't worry; we will take this step by step and make it as easy as possible.

So now that you understand why we are here and what we are going to cover, let's get started. If you already understand binary and hexadecimal, you can skip the next chapter and move straight to chapter 3. If you don't understand binary and hexadecimal, or if you want a refresher, grab your pencils and let's talk math.

Chapter 2

Math Time: A Review of Binary, Decimal, and Hexadecimal

Why do mathematicians get Christmas and Halloween confused?
Answer: Because Dec 25 = Oct 31 (hint: 011001)

The Secret to the Universe

I am going to let you in on a little secret, just for the purchase price of this book. Everyone always wants to know what the secret to the universe is. It is right here in this section. Anything you ever wanted to know is simplified right here; you just have to figure out how to decode it.

Simply stated, it either is or it isn't. That's where binary comes in.

All forms of data communications simply come down to a string of "0"s and "1"s. For a computer that is sending and receiving this information, it is not a problem at all. A computer can easily extrapolate the specific information based on where it resides in that string.

For us, on the other hand, that can be extremely difficult to do, especially when you may be looking at a string of 128 bits for a single address. So we convert this into something much easier to read for IPv6: hexadecimal characters.

You must understand hexadecimal when dealing with IPv6 addresses. This is where the first element of pain comes in for many people when working with IPv6. You may be familiar, and comfortable, looking at an IPv4 address. As soon as we convert it to hexadecimal, though, your blood pressure rises slightly, you feel your body temperature increase a little, and you may even get a slight headache.

Once you understand hexadecimal better, you will find IPv6 much easier to work with. IPv6 allows you to target a smaller area of the address for your attention and, with hexadecimal, you only have to deal with 4 bits at a time. This chapter will provide a quick review of binary, decimal, and hexadecimal numbering and how to convert between them.

Binary (Base 2)

At the most basic level, all communications across a network are in binary. Binary is pretty straightforward: yes or no, on or off, to be or not to be, "that is the question" (sorry, I digress). With binary, there is no middle area: it either is or it isn't.

Binary is simply represented by way of a single digit (known as a "bit") that is either a 0 (called "off") or 1 (called "on"). This is why it is referred to as base 2. A single digit can have only one of two values, 0 or 1.

All data transmissions are just a string of binary 1s and 0s.

The receiver of the message must be able to properly decode

the 1s and 0s to interpret the message. Different encoding methods define how these bits are represented, as a 1 or 0, during the transmission.

A very simple example of this is the "on-off keying" scheme used in some optical transmissions. It is simply light on or light off. If, during the bit time, the light is turned on, you are transmitting a 1. If the light is off, it represents a 0.

If an application is communicating across the network, the message being sent must be converted into the 1s and 0s. According to the Open System Interconnection (OSI) model, this translation process takes place at the presentation layer.

Just think of this conversion process as how we are going to "present" the data to the receiver, as 1s and 0s, so that the receiver can understand what we are sending. This is basically the language we will speak so that the receiver can understand what we are trying to communicate.

Two examples of this "language" in computer terms would be the American Standard Code for Information Interchange (ASCII) and the Extended Binary Coded Decimal Interchange Code (EBCDIC). The first one, as it states, is the "standard" language, and the second one was created by IBM. Each one of these defines how a character being transmitted is converted, or translated, into a stream of 1s and 0s.

For example:

ASCII   01000001 = "A" & 01100001 = "a"

EBCDIC   11000001 = "A" & 10000001 = "a"

You can see in this example that translating the message into the right language is very important to make sure that the correct message is received.

At the lower layers of the OSI model (2–4), the bits have specific purposes based on where they are located. Translation of these bits is not necessary, other than for our understanding or representation. At layer 3, where IPv6 lives, we have the source and destination addresses. To make these addresses easier to work with, we represent them as a decimal or hexadecimal value, but to the computers and networking devices the addresses are all just a string of 1s and 0s.

The basic element of converting binary values into another form is binary to decimal, so let's start there.

Decimal (Base 10)

Decimal is what we typically refer to as our "numbers." Where binary is base 2, decimal is base 10. Each individual digit can represent 1 of 10 values. Specifically, the digit can be a 0, 1, 2, 3, 4, 5, 6, 7, 8, or 9. After that, you must use two digits: 10, 11, 12, etc. Decimal is mostly used in IPv4 and is not too common in IPv6. Understanding it is important, though, so you can correctly translate between the two versions when planning a migration. Decimal is also used in some cases within IPv6 (such as ISATAP addressing).

Converting from binary to decimal is fairly easy. You give a decimal value to each bit in a binary string and simply add up the decimal value of each bit that is turned on. Starting from the least significant bit (on the far right), you assign a decimal value of "1" and simply double the decimal value for each more significant bit to the left.

bit		8	7	6	5	4	3	2	1
decimal value		128	64	32	16	8	4	2	1

binary	to	decimal	
0	=	0	
1	=	1	
10	=	2	(2 + 0)
11	=	3	(2 + 1)
100	=	4	(4 + 0)
101	=	5	(4 + 0 + 1)
110	=	6	(4 + 2 + 0)
111	=	7	(4 + 2 + 1)
1000	=	8	(8 + 0 + 0 + 0)

Fig 2.1

When you convert from binary to other values, such as octal or hexadecimal, you start out the same as converting to decimal. The difference is in how many bits can be used and what happens when you exhaust the ten decimal numbers (0–9) for a single character. So now, let's look at how that is dealt with in hexadecimal.

Hexadecimal (Base 16)

IPv6 addresses are represented in hexadecimal, so it is very important to understand how it works. When you understand this, it becomes much easier to work with IPv6 addressing, because you only have to deal with 4 bits at a time instead of the 8 bits at a time used by IPv4. That means we have only 16 values to focus on at a time instead of the 256 different values for an octet.

In hexadecimal, a single digit can have sixteen different values (base 16). How can you do that when there are only ten numbers? It's easy; once we run out of numbers, we switch to letters (a–f).

While binary is based on individual bits and decimal can continue indefinitely, hexadecimal is limited to blocks of 4 bits. This is because 4 bits gives you 16 total combinations. A byte is 8 bits long; therefore, 4 bits is half of a byte. This is called a "nibble" (yes, seriously).

Each hexadecimal value is a representation of a 4-bit nibble.

Binary	Decimal	Hexadecimal
0000	0	0
0001	1	1
0010	2	2
0011	3	3
0100	4	4
0101	5	5
0110	6	6
0111	7	7
1000	8	8
1001	9	9
1010	10	a
1011	11	b
1100	12	c
1101	13	d
1110	14	e
1111	15	f

Fig 2.2

When you work with larger values, using hexadecimal makes the values much easier to work with. Everything can be broken down into one of the 16 values shown here. For example, the binary value of 10010100 would be 148 in decimal, or 94 (pronounced as "nine four," not "ninety-four") in hexadecimal. Just imagine trying to convert the following:

00100000000000001000011011011100000000000010101
10000000000000000010000001000110100010101011011
1111111111110011110001001101010111100

We'll look at what all of that means in the next chapter.

Once you understand the basic mechanics, you can get into the details. Now that we can think in binary, decimal, and hexadecimal, let's put it to work on something that is useful. It's an easy way to get free drinks. (Well, in certain places, but we won't go there for now.) It is also necessary in identifying and understanding addresses. In the next chapter, we will look at how an IPv6 address is represented.

Chapter 3

Now That's Scary Looking: The IPv6 Address Format

> *I need a proctologist; I think there is a problem with my colon. Oh wait, that's a semicolon.*

A Step at a Time

The very first part of understanding IPv6 is being able to look at the address without cringing and having your eyes gloss over. Believe it or not, that's actually possible to do. The formatting of the address was specifically designed to make the 128 bits easy to work with, compared with alternative formats.

Everything that we are going to do going forward is based on this address. Once you understand how it is formatted, you can easily identify specific components of it relating to whatever task is currently at hand. This applies to routing, security, Quality of Service, etc.

If we don't take this basic step to understand how the address is presented, it will just look like a string of cypher-text and everything else will not make much sense.

In this chapter, we will start with a complete 128-bit binary address and then format it based on four simple steps.

Address Representation

Let's take a look at how the IPv6 address is represented to make it much easier to work with.

In chapter 2, we discussed how all information is transmitted across the network from one device to another as binary. This is easy for the computers and infrastructure equipment to identify and process but not very easy for a human to deal with. So the first step is converting the addresses from binary into something a little easier to read.

In IPv4, this conversion was done by taking the 32-bit address, breaking it into four equal octets (8-bit group), and converting each binary octet into decimal. Instead of trying to digest the entire 32-bit address, you only have to focus on 1 byte at a time. The decimal representation is fairly simple because you have only 256 combinations that you can get out of 8 binary bits, giving you a decimal range from 0 to 255 (00000000–11111111 in binary).

Following this same process would be more difficult for IPv6 because the address space itself is four times the size of IPv4. It could be done, but a much better approach was chosen. Let's look at this in four simple steps:

1. Segment
2. Represent
3. Simplify
4. Consolidate

Let's start with the example I showed you in the last chapter—an IPv6 address in its basic format (binary):

0010000000000001000011011011100000000000000000
0000000000000000000010000000000000000000000000
0000000000000000000000000000000000000000000001

Looking at this too long will make your eyes start playing tricks on you. So let's make it better.

Step 1: Segment

For the first step, you divide the 128 bits of the sample address into eight equal segments of 16 bits each. Each of these 16-bit segments will be separated by colons.

Why colons? Because we typically use a device's MAC address to come up with the host address ("interface_ID"). Hey look at that, MAC addresses are in hexadecimal and typically delimited by colons. It makes the format consistent.

0010000000000001 : 0000110110111000 : 0000000000000000 : 0000000000000001 :
0000000000000000 : 0000000000000000 : 0000000000000000 : 0000000000000001

Fig 3.1

Note: What is the colon key? It is the shift/semicolon key. Watch out for typos.

Step 2: Represent

If you represented each segment as a decimal value, as in IPv4, you would have a lot more difficulty doing the conversion because 16 binary bits gives you 65,536 decimal values. To make it much easier, in IPv6 we represent each segment by its hexadecimal value. So the next step will be to break the address segments into nibbles and use each nibble's hexadecimal value. (You can refer to the chart in chapter 2 if you have difficulty with this.)

```
  2    0    0    1  : 0    d    b    8  : 0    0    0    0  : 0    0    0    1  :
0010 0000 0000 0001 : 0000 1101 1011 1000 : 0000 0000 0000 0000 : 0000 0000 0000 0001 :
  0    0    0    0  : 0    0    0    0  : 0    0    0    0  : 0    0    0    1
0000 0000 0000 0000 : 0000 0000 0000 0000 : 0000 0000 0000 0000 : 0000 0000 0000 0001
```

2001:0db8:0000:0001:0000:0000:0000:0001

Fig 3.2

Step 3: Simplify

Now even in this format there is a lot to look at and it can still look confusing. The next step is to simplify the representation by eliminating leading zeros. Because we know that there are 16 bits between every two colons (as long as there is anything between the colons), and the systems read the address starting with the least significant bit (on the right), we can omit the most significant zeros (on the left) between the colons.

2001:0db8:0000:0001:0000:0000:0000:0001
becomes
2001:db8:0:1:0:0:0:1

Step 4: Consolidate

Finally, we can consolidate consecutive segments that are all zeros. Consecutive segments of 0s can be consolidated by using two colons with nothing between them: "::". You can do this only once within an address, though, because the systems must be able to determine how many bits are being consolidated between the colons. They do this by seeing how many bits are otherwise represented in front of and after the "::".

2001:db8:0:1:0:0:0:1

becomes

2001:db8:0:1::1

In this example, 64 bits are represented in front of the double colon and 16 bits are represented after the double colon. If you subtract the 80 represented bits (64 + 16) from the 128 bits of the entire address space, you can determine that 48 bits (128 – 80 = 48) of zeros are consolidated within the double colon. This consolidation is used very frequently in IPv6 addressing. Here are some other examples (we will talk about what these specific addresses are later):

FF02:0000:0000:0000:0000:0000:0000:0001 = **FF02::1**   (all nodes multicast)
FF02:0000:0000:0000:0000:0000:0000:0002 = **FF02::1**   (all routers multicast)
FF02:0000:0000:0000:0000:0000:0001:0002 = **FF02::1:2**   (DHCP servers/relays)
0000:0000:0000:0000:0000:0000:0000:0001 = **::1**   (local loopback address)
0000:0000:0000:0000:0000:0000:0000:0000 = **::**   ("unspecified)

Fig 3.3

Now, doesn't that look much easier?

Where Is the Subnet Mask?

"What is this cider thing I keep hearing about? Is it pear or apple? Are we having a party?"

Not "cider" as in "apple cider" or "pear cider." It's CIDR. It stands for Classless Inter-Domain Routing. It was introduced as "Supernetting" in 1992 and then updated as "Classless Inter-Domain Routing" in 1993. It was also updated again in 2006.

CIDR allows us to break the address into two primary elements, the network address and the host address (called the "prefix" and "interface_ID" in IPv6).

The sending host and all intermediate routers must be able to identify which bits of an address represent the network so they can decide how to forward the packet. We could simply split the 128-bit address in half and say that the first 64 bits are always the prefix and the last 64 bits are always the host. The problem with that is that we would possibly have to store all 64-bit prefixes in all of the routers.

The 64-bit prefix space gives the possibility for 2,305,843,009,213,693,952 global prefixes. Imagine having to store that table in every one of your routers and search through it if you need to find a specific prefix.

CIDR allows you to simply identify what range of bits, starting with the most significant bit, identifies the network prefix. This is what allows the concept of "supernetting" or aggregating many prefixes within one entry. CIDR is represented as a forward slash immediately following the address, followed by a number identifying the number of prefix bits. Let's look at a couple of examples:

2001:db8:1ac:30f:234:56ff:fe78:9abc**/64**

> The "/64" identifies the first 64 bits as the prefix. The routing table in this case would show "2001:db8:1ac:30f::/64".

2001:db8:1ac:30f::/56 (Okay, this is a tricky example.)
Keep in mind that between every two colons there
are 16 bits, excluding the "::", and we can eliminate only *leading* zeros. So this address is really
"2001:0db8:01ac:030f::/56". The first 56 bits com-
prise the prefix (2001:0db8:01ac:03, as the final "0f"
are just the remaining 8 bits of the fourth segment).
In the routing table, any unused bits are set to zero, so
the entry would be "2001:db8:1ac:300::**/56**".

Question: Why wouldn't it be "2001:db8:1ac:3::/56"?

Answer: Because you can omit only leading zeros,
not trailing zeros. 2001:db8:1ac:3:: would be
2001:0db8:01ac:0003::, so the first 56 bits would be
2001:0db8:01a:00 . . .

A few other examples:

2001:db8:1ac::/48

2001:db8:100::/40

2001:db8::/32

2000::/3 (This is the range assigned for global unicast
addresses.)

Which would you rather look at and have to work with?

0010000000000001000011011011100000000000000000
0000000000000000000100000000000000000000000000
0000000000000000000000000000000000000000000001
/64

or

2001:0db8:0000:0001:0000:0000:0000:0001/64

or

2001:db8:0:1::1/64

Now the mystery about how the address looks should be gone. At this point, besides how to represent it, all we know about this address is that the first 64 bits are typically the prefix and the last 64 bits are typically the interface_ID of the host. In the next chapter, we will further break down each of the subcomponents of the address and see how they are assigned.

Chapter 4

We're Going Global, Baby: Types of IPv6 Addresses and Address Allocation

What is the difference between a unicast and a multicast? What the hell happened to broadcasts?

Address Your Address

The IPv6 address structure has many little subcomponents contained within it: what type of address it is, each of the assigning authorities, the organization's address, and the subnetwork within the organization. It also has the individual host that the address is assigned to, or the group it is going out to.

Understanding this structure will help you in many ways, such as being able to create an addressing scheme for your organization. It also helps you identify commonalities or points of reference within an address that you can use when creating security policies. Understanding some of the special address types may keep you from beating your head against the wall trying to figure out why they are there.

If any of the elements in an address are misrepresented, any number of problems can occur. You can have security breaches in your network. You might end up with hosts or entire network segments that cannot communicate. You could possibly have the entire organization cut off from the outside world.

In this chapter, we will cover the types of addresses (unicast and multicast), along with special types of unicast addresses. We will also see how addresses are allocated all the way from the Internet Assigned Numbers Authority (IANA) out to the end hosts. Let's start by looking at the different types of addresses.

Unicast vs. Multicast (And What Happened to Broadcasts?)

Unfortunately, we are not here to talk about sushi, though I will say that uni (the California sea urchin) is one of my favorites, if it is fresh.

In relation to our addresses, the prefix "uni" means one, like unicycle (or unibrow). I've heard people try to describe a unicycle as "a bicycle with one wheel," but that would be incorrect because the prefix "bi" in bicycle implies that it has two.

Anyway, with the prefix of "uni" meaning one, a unicast address is typically referred to as a one-to-one address. Legitimate source addresses are always a unicast address because the packet is sent from a single host. When the destination address is a unicast address, the packet is going to only one host.

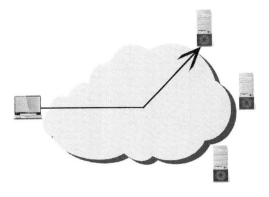

Fig 4.1

An example of a unicast communication would be watching an "on-demand" movie. You request the movie, and the server sends the video stream to your set-top box only. If other people want to watch the same movie, multiple streams would be sent out, one to each box. This, of course, could consume a lot of bandwidth.

"Multi" is an abbreviation of multiple, meaning more than one. So a multicast address would be an address that goes to more than one destination host, also referred to as a "one-to-many" communication. In IPv6, this type of address is identified by the first byte, as you will see in the next section.

Traffic directed to multicast destinations will be replicated, as necessary, and forwarded out along all paths required to reach the hosts that want to receive it.

Fig 4.2

This is the way the normal channel programming is typically forwarded from a cable provider. The channel video is sent out as one stream. Each intermediate device will replicate and forward it toward all the destinations that are viewing it.

Okay, so What about Broadcasts?

The term "broadcast" has a couple of meanings.

In one sense, it means something that is sent once and everyone receives, within a specific range called a "broadcast domain." For example, if you go to a rock concert and you are anywhere in or around the venue, you will hear the band. I could play a note once and it would be broadcast through the speakers so everyone within the venue would hear it. Granted, you may not be listening to it, but you would still hear it. I could always turn the amplifiers up. . . . As Nigel Tufnel said in *This Is Spinal Tap*, "These go to eleven."

Another meaning of "broadcast" is a specific type of address. A "broadcast" address is an address that has all bits turned on. In IPv4, the broadcast address is 255.255.255.255 (11111111.11 111111.11111111.11111111). At layer 2 (the data-link layer), the broadcast MAC address is ff:ff:ff:ff:ff:ff (11111111111111111111 1111111111111111111111111111).

One of the phrases I hear a lot is "There are no broadcasts in IPv6." This is either correct or incorrect depending on your meaning of the term "broadcast."

There is no address in IPv6 that has all 128 bits turned on. There is, however, an address that behaves like a broadcast. If you send packets to this address, every IPv6 host within the "broadcast domain" will pick them up. This is done by using a specific multicast address called the "all nodes multicast." Even though all of the bits are not turned on (actually, most of them are off), the packet will be handled like a broadcast address.

Note: The term "broadcast domain" refers to all the nodes that will receive a broadcast. This includes all nodes up to and including a router. Routers will receive and process broadcast messages but will not forward them, except in a few specially configured cases. Switches, by default, forward multicast and broadcast frames out of all interfaces except the interface the frame was received on. You can separate switch ports into different broadcast domains by configuring virtual LANs (VLANs) and assigning the switch ports to their respective VLAN.

Five Types of Addresses

That's all cool, unicast, multicast, no broadcast, I get it, but how do we identify which type an address is?

The high-order bits at the beginning of the address are used to identify the type of address.

According to the "IP Version 6 Addressing Architecture" RFC (4291), there are five types of addresses. This gives us a starting point from which to work. Further classifications have been defined for specific purposes, and we will discuss those as well. First, though, let's look at what the RFC gives us.

Unspecified	::/128	000...0 (128 bits)
Loopback	::1/128	000...1 (128 bits)
Multicast	FF00::/8	1111 1111 ...
Link_Local Unicast	FE80::/10	1111 1110 10...
Global Unicast	Everything Else	

Fig 4.3

Unspecified

"Unspecified" means all bits are set to zero (0:0:0:0:0:0:0:0, or simply ::/128). The unspecified address cannot be assigned to any host. This address indicates the absence of any specific address and, therefore, cannot be forwarded by a host or router.

It is also used to represent the default route in routing tables. Similar to IPv4, where the specification for a default route is an address of all 0s with an all 0 mask (0.0.0.0 0.0.0.0), the IPv6 default route is also represented as all 0s with a CIDR prefix length of 0 (::/0).

Here is an example of configuring default routes on a Cisco router.

ip route ***0.0.0.0 0.0.0.0*** 10.1.2.3 (IPv4)

ipv6 route ***::/0*** 2001:db8:1:2::1 (IPv6)

Loopback

The loopback address is a unicast that allows a node to send a packet to itself. This has the same purpose as the IPv4 loopback address of 127.0.0.1. In IPv6, the loopback address has the 128-bit assignment of ::1/128. This can be used for testing the sending and receiving abilities of a host without going through a network.

Multicast

Multicast addresses, as stated earlier, are destination addresses that may be received by more than one destination node. Multicast addresses are identified by having the first 8 bits turned on (FFxx). The entire first 16-bit segment of the address is used to control the address.

The last byte of the first segment provides the control information.

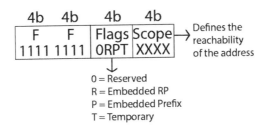

Fig 4.4

Flags:

The third nibble from the left contains the address flags. The least significant bit of the flag segment, the "T" bit, identifies whether this is a permanently assigned multicast address (0), in an RFC for example, or a temporary address (1) that is assigned and managed by a network administrator.

The second bit, the "P" bit, identifies whether the address contains an embedded unicast prefix within the multicast group ID. This would be done when creating a multicast address that is globally unique because it contains an organization's global unicast prefix within the address. If the bit is off (0), no prefix is embedded. If it is on (1), there is an embedded prefix.

The third bit identifies whether a multicast rendezvous point (RP) host ID is embedded within the address. This may be used in a Protocol Independent Multicast Sparse Mode (PIM-SM) deployment. The embedded RP allows a multicast listener to join a group without having any knowledge of where the source server for the stream is located. If the "R" bit is off (0), no RP is included. If it is on (1), the RP's host ID is included. This also requires that the "P" bit is on and a prefix is embedded. The designated router (DR) attempting to join a group will get the RP's address by combining the embedded prefix with the RP's embedded host ID.

The fourth bit is reserved for future use. Currently, it is always off.

Scope:

The least significant nibble identifies the "scope" or reachability of the address. This identifies, in part, how a router will handle a packet that is sent to a multicast destination. For example, if the scope is 2 (0010), called link-local, a router will receive and process the packet but will never forward it beyond the "link."

With 4 bits, you get 16 total values, and most of these are unassigned. In reality, we typically use only 2 of the 8 possible scope IDs. These are the link-local scope (2) and global scope (E).

> 0   reserved
> 1   interface-local scope
> 2   link-local scope
> 3   reserved
> 4   admin-local scope
> 5   site-local scope
> 6   unassigned
> 7   unassigned
> 8   organization-local scope
> 9   unassigned
> a   unassigned
> b   unassigned
> c   unassigned
> d   unassigned
> e   global scope
> f   reserved

Interface-local (1) stays contained within a single interface on a node. This is just a loopback multicast transmission.

Link-local (2) stays contained within the "link." Basically, this can span the broadcast domain, up to and including routers, but not through them. A lot of management traffic uses this scope.

Admin-local (4) is designed to allow the scope to be administratively configured. This is the smallest scope, excluding interface-local and link-local.

Site-local (5) is intended to stay contained within a single site.

Organization-local (8) is intended to extend across multiple sites that are all part of the same organization.

Global (E) can span as far as multicast is supported. Assuming that all the internet carriers support multicast, a global scope would allow someone to set up a stream in the US, for example, that people in China, Germany, or wherever could receive. This would typically also require the embedded RP address for join reachability.

Some common multicast addresses include the following:

FF02::1   This is the "all nodes multicast" address. It is the IPv6 equivalent to the IPv4 broadcast address (255.255.255.255). This address will be picked up and processed by every IPv6 node within the broadcast domain.

The "FF" at the beginning of the address identifies it as a "multicast" address. The flags nibble of "0" tells us that it is a standard address. The scope "2" tells us that it stays local to the link. (The "FF02::" prefix is called a "link-local multicast" prefix.) Last of all is the multicast group ID (the remaining bits of "1").

This specific address is used, for example, by routers to advertise themselves to all IPv6 nodes off the router's interface.

FF02::2   This address is the "all routers multicast" address. The only difference between this address and the previous one is the multicast group ID of "::2". It is still a link-local multicast, but it will be picked up only by routers on the link.

FF02::1:ff::   This is the "solicited-node multicast" prefix. It is used as a way to come up with a layer 2 multicast MAC address to communicate with a node on a network segment when the sender doesn't know the MAC address of the node it is trying to reach. We will look at this more in chapter 6 when we talk about neighbor discovery (ND) communications.

Link-Local Unicast

Any interface that is enabled for IPv6 will automatically be assigned a link-local unicast address that starts with "fe8". The reserved space for these is FE80::/10. This address is used for control communications, such as exchanging routing information, with other devices on the same link. These addresses are almost never used by the users or administrators.

You can change these addresses on the interfaces, if you want, but you cannot remove them without removing IPv6 from the interface.

Fig 4.5

In figure 4.5, you can see that not only are the network segments using the same prefix, but the routers can have the exact same address on different interfaces. Nope, there's no routing happening here. It is impossible for a router to use this type of address as a destination to help you reach a remote host on another network segment.

Link-local addressing does not even show up in the routing tables. This is because you have the same network prefix (fe80::/10) on every interface.

If you want to manually communicate with a host on your network segment by its link-local address, you must tell the sending host specifically what interface to use for the communication.

Global Unicast

Everything else has been, technically, designated as global unicast addressing.

Okay, so the term "global" is actually a limiting term by definition. Specifically, it would limit you to "worldwide" or to a "celestial body," but that's not how they meant it. I think a better term would be "universal," but they didn't ask for my opinion.

Basically, this means that every address from this space is

globally unique from every other host address. These addresses may be reachable by any other host without any form of address translation necessary.

To maintain control and still allow for future refinement, different address blocks have been reserved and allocated for specific purposes. Based on this, the 2000::/3 prefix has been designated as the prefix for global unicast addressing.

2000::/3 = global unicast

The top-level organization responsible for the assignment of address space is the Internet Assigned Numbers Authority (IANA). Even though IANA is the supreme addressing authority, it gives the responsibility of the actual address block assignments to organizations called Regional Internet Registries (RIRs). The five RIRs are responsible for the allocations at regional levels, as shown in figure 4.6.

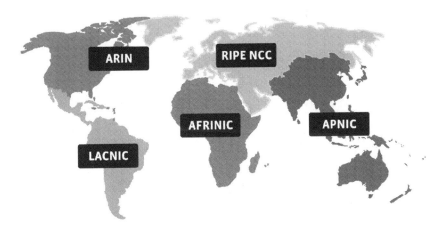

Fig 4.6

Over the years, IANA has made several modifications to the allocations. Initially, it assigned /23 blocks to the RIRs, with more blocks being allocated as needed. In 2006, IANA standardized the block assignments to the RIRs, basing them on /12 prefixes.

Here is the current prefix space allocated to each of the RIRs, along with the date of the allocation.

ARIN (American Registry for Internet Numbers)
2001:0400::/23	July 1, 1999
2001:1800::/23	April 1, 2003
2001:4800::/23	August 24, 2004
2610:0000::/23	November 17, 2005
2620:0000::/23	September 12, 2006
2600::/12	October 3, 2006

APNIC (Asia-Pacific Network Information Centre)
2001:0200::/23	July 1, 1999
2001:0c00::/23	May 2, 2002
2001:0e00::/23	January 1, 2003
2001:4400::/23	June 11, 2004
2001:8000::/19	November 30, 2004
2001:a000::/20	November 30, 2004
2001:b000::/20	March 8. 2006
2400::/12	October 3, 2006

RIPE NCC (Réseaux IP Européens Network Coordination Centre)
2001:0600::/23	July 1, 1999
2001:0800::/23	May 2, 2002
2001:0a00::/23	November 2, 2002
2001:1400::/23	February 1, 2003
2001:1600::/23	July 1, 2003
2001:1a00::/23	January 1, 2004
2001:1c00::/22	May 4, 2004
2001:2000::/20	May 4, 2004
2001:3000::/21	May 4, 2004
2001:3800::/22	May 4, 2004
2001:4000::/23	June 11, 2004
2001:4600::/23	August 17, 2004
2001:4a00::/23	October 15, 2004
2001:4c00::/23	December 17, 2004
2001:5000::/20	September 10, 2004
2003::/18	January 12, 2005
2a00::/12	October 3, 2006

LACNIC (Latin America and Caribbean Network Information Centre)
       2001:1200::/23   November 1, 2002
       2800::/12   October 3, 2006
AFRINIC (African Network Information Center)
       2001:4200::/23   June 1, 2004
       2c00::/12   October 3, 2006

Fig 4.7

So what's the deal with all of these allocations? The purpose of the disbursement of addresses this way is to distribute control over the assignments to different regions of the world.

The Local Internet Registry (LIR) layer comprises the service providers that are assigning addresses to organizations or users. The "EU" is the end user of the address. This could be an organization or it could be an actual user, as in the case of a home network.

This allocation structure was designed to restrict the growth of the internet routing table. In IPv6, the prefix can be 64 bits, and longer in some cases. The 64 bits give you up to 18,446,744,073,709,551,616 total prefix possibilities.

The initial concept was that end users could not get their own address prefix and would basically be a subnet of the service provider (LIR). In this case, only the LIR prefixes would be in the internet routing tables.

The initial LIR allocation is a 32-bit assignment from the RIR's address space. Even at 32 bits, you could have up to 4,294,967,296 total prefixes. That would be the same as having every individual IPv4 host address listed in the routing table. Realistically, though, the number of service providers with 32-bit prefixes is very small compared with the number of end user organizations.

The big problem with this scheme is that all end users would be tied to the service provider that assigned the address space to them. From a home or small office perspective, this is not a big deal and is the way it typically works.

If you are a large business, however, this scheme has much larger issues.

Let's say you are someone like eBay, for example. It would be very difficult to set up and use a redundancy solution that involved more than one service provider because you would be assigned, and required to use, address space from each provider.

That, itself, could create big reachability problems with asymmetric routing issues and firewall state-table management. What if you want to switch service providers? You would have to release the prefix assigned by the first provider and reassign every one of your addresses with the prefix from the new provider. This would also involve changing anything that referred to the old prefix, including access lists, firewall rules, and DNS.

In 2009, the RIRs started allowing end users to get provider-independent address space as long as they meet certain conditions. The primary reason for this is to allow the use of multihoming, so the EU organization can connect to two or more service providers and be able to control its own addressing. This address space can be applied for and received from the RIR directly instead of from the LIR.

Do You Have a Reservation?

Blocks of address space have been reserved, for different purposes, and are therefore unassignable publicly. Here are a couple of the reservations; I will give more detail later on some of the specifics.

2001:db8::/32

"I lost my phone number; can I have yours?"

Have you ever given a fake phone number to a girl, or guy, whom you met but didn't really like, so he or she couldn't really call you? I actually gave the number "619-555-1212" to someone before. I thought she must have been really stupid not to realize that it was a bogus number with a "555" prefix, but the joke was on me. It turns out that 555-1212 is the information phone number for any area code in the United States. When she called it, she just asked for my name, and they gave her my real number because I was not unlisted at the time.

Other than the "information" phone number, "555" is an unassigned prefix that is used in movies, television shows, etc., especially since the band Tommy Tutone became popular with a song called "867-5309/Jenny" and people who had that phone number started getting a lot of phone calls looking for a girl named "Jenny."

2001:db8::/32 is to network prefixes what "555" is to phone prefixes. It is a specially assigned prefix for use in documentation.

2001:0000::/32

This prefix is reserved for nodes doing Teredo tunneling. We'll take a look at this in chapter 8.

2002::/16

This prefix is reserved for nodes that are part of a 6to4 tunneled network. We will see this in chapter 8 as well.

The Host with the Most

Okay, so we've looked at how prefixes are allocated from IANA to the EU—but what about the hosts? Everything up to this point has been based on the network prefix. Now we have the host addresses to deal with.

IPv6 is designed to allow a host to be able to create its own host address, called the "interface_ID," based on its unique MAC address. Once an address is chosen, the host will start a process called duplicate address detection (DAD) to verify that the address is not currently in use by someone else. This is done by passing neighbor discovery messages through the network with the Internet Message Control Protocol (ICMP).

We will discuss ICMP messages in chapter 6.

EUI-64

So, let's get this straight. The total v6 address is 128 bits, check. The first 64 bits are assigned as the network prefix, check. The rest of the address, 64 bits, is used to identify the host and is automatically determined by using the MAC address of the host, check.

Wait, what? The MAC address is 48 bits, but the host portion of the address is 64 bits?

What happens to the rest of the bits?

EUI-64 stands for 64-bit extended unique identifier. It is simply a way to expand the 48-bit MAC address of a host for use as the 64-bit interface_ID.

First, think of the format of the MAC address. You have 48 bits that are based on two 24-bit elements. The first 24 bits (the most significant) are called the OUI (organizationally unique identifier), also commonly referred to as the vendor_ID, which is assigned to the manufacturer by the Institute of Electrical and Electronics Engineers (IEEE). This element ensures the uniqueness of MAC addresses assigned by different manufacturers, such as Apple, Dell, and HP.

The last 24 bits (the least significant) are the extended system identifier (ESI), which is uniquely assigned by the manufacturer for each MAC address. This system allows a manufacturer to be able to assign 16,777,216 unique MAC addresses before having to get a new OUI from IEEE.

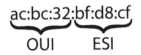

Fig 4.8

One other element of the MAC address, used by EUI-64, is the use of the 2 least significant bits of the first byte.

```
a   c : b   c : 3   2 : b   f : d   8 : c   f
1010 1100 : 1011 1100 : 0011 0010 : 1011 1111 : 1101 1000 : 1100 1111
  U/L   I/G
```

Fig 4.9

Bit 1 is the "I/G" (individual/group) bit and is used to determine whether the MAC address is a unicast ("individual") address or a multicast ("group") address. If bit 1 is off (0), then the address is to an individual host (unicast). If the bit is on (1), then the address is to a group of hosts (multicast or broadcast).

Bit 2 is the "U/L" (universal/local) bit and is used to determine the administrative authority, and the uniqueness, of the address. If this bit is off (0), the address is universally unique, and if the bit is on (1), the address is locally administered and therefore considered to be only locally unique. Whenever IEEE assigns an OUI to a manufacturer, both of these bits are always off.

In EUI-64, the "extended" part is to extend the existing host MAC address from the 48 bits to 64 bits in order to fill the address space. This is simply done by stuffing a fixed 16-bit pattern of 1111 1111 1111 1110 (FFFE) between the OUI and ESI of the host's MAC address.

Because we are now in effect modifying the host ID, the U/L bit is also flipped. For example, if a host has a MAC address of ac:bc:32:bf:d8:cf, the resulting EUI-64 interface_ID for IPv6 will be aebc:32ff:febf:d8cf.

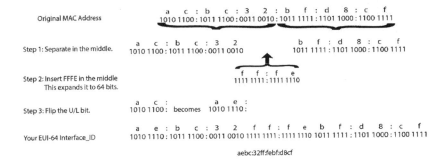

Fig 4.10

The major benefit of using EUI-64 addressing is that it is automatic and unique, based on the fact that your MAC address already must be unique for layer 2 communications to work. With stateless autoconfiguration, just about any idiot can connect to an IPv6 network by simply plugging in a cable and can be reasonably assured there will be no addressing conflicts.

Dynamic Host Configuration Protocol (DHCP)

Using DHCP is called "stateful autoconfiguration" because the address-to-host assignments are tracked (stateful) and may be logged and archived. In normal stateless autoconfiguration, there is no tracking of which host specifically is using which address at a given time. With DHCP, this information can be maintained.

IPv6 was designed to work as a stateless autoconfiguration protocol, and that is still its initial preferred behavior. Flags in the Router Advertisement messages can tell the requesting host to use DHCP to get an address or just use DHCP for additional information such as the DNS servers.

Usually, when a host connects to the network and brings up its interface, the host will attempt to discover whether there is a DHCP server, which it does by sending out a solicitation.

Fig 4.11

If a DHCP server receives the solicitation, it will reply by sending back an advertisement offering its services.

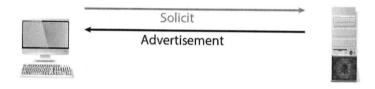

Fig 4.12

When the client receives the advertisement from the DHCP server, it will then send a request message asking for an address.

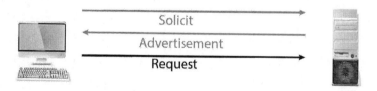

Fig 4.13

Finally, the DHCP server will respond with an Acknowledge message that will include the address for the client. It could provide additional information as well, such as the default gateway to use, the DNS servers to use, or DHCP options.

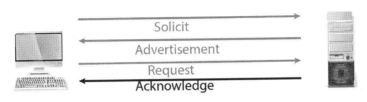

Fig 4.14

Other Methods

There are, of course, other methods for assigning the interface_ ID of the address, including the software making a "random" assignment. You could manually assign the address. There is also a process for cryptographically generated addresses.

If you want to know more about these, go to http://v6book. com/extras.

From I to H (IANA to the Host)

Okay, so let's review the address allocation from IANA to the end host. To avoid conflict with any real addressing, and to follow the usage of the "documentation only" address space, we will use a fictitious RIR that we will call "KULLNIC." IANA has specified the prefix 2000::/3 (*001. ....*) for global address assignments and has assigned, for our virtual example, a /12 prefix of 2000::/12 (001*0 0000 0000* ....) to the RIR "KULLNIC."

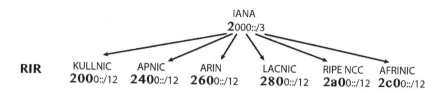

Fig 4.15

As an RIR, KULLNIC makes assignments to Local Internet Registries (LIRs, or ISPs) and, in some cases, to end user organizations (EUs). In this example, let's say that KULLNIC has a service provider customer called Adagio Networks and assigns to it the /32-bit prefix of 2001:db8::/32 (0010 0000 0000 **0001:0000 1101 1011 1000::**).

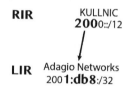

Fig 4.16

The "site prefix" space is 48 bits, so Adagio Networks is going to take one /48 prefix (2001:db8:1::/48) for its own internal network use and assign other prefixes to its EU customers. Adagio Networks has an end user customer called T6 Solutions and assigns the next subnetwork of its /32 prefix, 2001:db8:2::/48 (0010 0000 0000 0001:0000 1101 1011 1000:**0000 0000 0000 0010::**) to T6 Solutions.

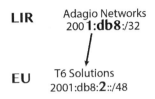

LIR   Adagio Networks
             200**1:db8:**/32

EU   T6 Solutions
             2001:db8:**2**::/48

Fig 4.17

Using the assigned 48-bit "site prefix," T6 Solutions now has 16 bits that it can use to assign network prefixes to its individual networks. This gives T6 Solutions the ability to assign up to 65,536 unique network addresses to its internal networks. The first network can be 2001:db8:2:1::/64, the second 2001:db8:2:2/64, etc., up to 2001:db8:2:ffff::/64. Each node on each network can use its MAC address to create its own host ID and have a unique host address that is potentially reachable from anywhere.

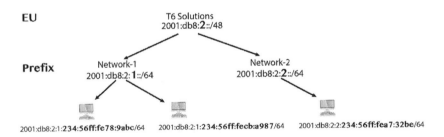

Fig 4.18

The hosts within the EU can use their MAC address to create their EUI-64 interface_ID. Now we have complete addresses and can easily identify the different elements of the address.

Wow, that was a lot of information. Now you should understand IPv6 addressing. You should be able to look at any IPv6
address and be able to identify a lot of information about it.

We need to see how this address gets used by your computers
and networks. In the next chapter, we will look at the layer 3
IPv6 encapsulation header, along with its extension headers.

Chapter 5

We're Gonna Need a Bigger Box: The IPv6 Encapsulation Header

> *How big was the largest envelope in the world?*
> *Answer: As of 2017, it was 23.93 m (73 ft. 6 in.) long and 13.5 m (44 ft. 3 in.) wide. (And you still couldn't fold it in half eight times.)*

Your Virtual Envelope

Okay, so we talked about that big address, what it's for, and how it gets allocated and assigned. What about how we use and transport it?

Now that we have this big address figured out, we need to be able to provide the address to the devices that will be helping us reach the destination. You can't send a letter through the mail without first putting it in an envelope and providing the addresses. This is where we get into encapsulation headers. They are your virtual envelope.

On an envelope, you have specific places for the information needed to forward it: a place for your return (source) address, a place for the recipient's (destination) address, a place for the postage, etc.

Without being able to direct your packets, you can't communicate. It would be like writing a letter and just dropping it in the mail without an envelope.

When you understand encapsulation headers, though, you can really start to use IPv6.

In this chapter, we are going to break down the IP encapsulation header to see how it is more streamlined than in IPv4. We will take a look at each of the fields of the base header. Then we will see what the extension headers are.

The IPv6 Header

IPv4 Header

Offsets Octet		0	1	2	3
Octet	Bit	00 01 02 03 04 05 06 07	08 09 10 11 12 13 14 15	16 17 18 19 20 21 22 23	24 25 26 27 28 29 30 31
0	0	Version	IHL	Type of Service	Total Length
4	32	Identification		Flags	Fragment Offset
8	64	Time to Live	Protocol	Header Checksum	
12	96	Source IP Address			
16	128	Destination IP Address			
20	160	Options			

IPv6 Header

Offsets Octet		0	1	2	3
Octet	Bit	00 01 02 03 04 05 06 07	08 09 10 11 12 13 14 15	16 17 18 19 20 21 22 23	24 25 26 27 28 29 30 31
0	0	Version	Traffic Class	Flow Label	
4	32	Payload Length		Next Header	Hop Limit
8	64	Source IP Address			
24	192	Destination IP Address			

Fig 5.1

In IPv4, a host can simply look at bytes 12 through 15 of the IP header and know that it is the sender's address and that bytes 16 through 19 are the destination address. This is based on the address size being 32 bits.

Because IPv6 addresses are four times the size, this byte space recognition will not work.

As a necessity, the header format had to be modified. We already had several years of experience working with IPv4 and had a good idea of what worked and what could be improved. This created a great opportunity to fix a few issues. The encapsulation header was modified to not only allow the larger address space but also streamline the process of handling and forwarding the traffic.

During this modification, only one field, the Version field, was left untouched. Everything else has been renamed, moved, modified, or eliminated. Only one new field was added, the Flow Label field.

The IPv6 base header is a simplified header that contains only the basic information needed to process the packet. Any additional information needed, such as fragment reassembly information, can be attached as an extension to the base header. Extension header encapsulations are used only when needed and do not consume any space or resources otherwise.

The rest of this section explains the format and purpose of each field of the layer 3 IPv6 encapsulation header: Version, Traffic Class, Flow Label, Payload Length, Next Header, Hop Limit, Source Address, and Destination Address.

Version

This field is the first 4 bits. It identifies the version of Internet Protocol being used and, therefore, what information follows. In IPv6, this is set to 0110 (6).

Traffic Class

This 8-bit field is the renamed Type of Service field from IPv4. As the name implies, it is used to define the "class" of traffic that can be used as part of the Quality of Service (QoS) implementation. This helps ensure that more critical traffic is delivered efficiently and that you don't have your phone call dropped because someone is downloading a file somewhere. The Traffic Class field can be set by the source, but it can also be changed by intermediate devices in the network.

Even though the entire byte is called the "Traffic Class," it is actually divided into two different parts. The most significant 6 bits are called the Differentiated Services Code Point (DSCP), or "DiffServ," and the least significant 2 bits are currently unused but considered for Explicit Congestion Notification (ECN) in the event that the devices in the network would be capable of supporting them.

The 6 DSCP bits allow for sixty-four different classifications of the traffic that can be assigned by upper layer services for data handling. These are subdivided into three pools, as identified by the least significant 1 or 2 bits of the DSCP bits.

The current standard assignments include eight code points called Class Selectors (CS) that are assigned for backward compatibility with the old "IP Precedence" (the most significant 3 bits of the IPv6 Type of Service [ToS] field). These are identified by having the least significant 3 bits of the DSCP set to off (xxx000), leaving the 3 most significant bits for CS identification. The remaining standard assignments include twelve levels of Assured Forwarding (AF), one Expedited Forwarding (EF), and one value for the identification of voice traffic.

Name	Binary	Reference
CS0	000000	RFC-2474
CS1	001000	RFC-2474
CS2	010000	RFC-2474
CS3	011000	RFC-2474
CS4	100000	RFC-2474
CS5	101000	RFC-2474
CS6	110000	RFC-2474
CS7	111000	RFC-2474
AF11	001010	RFC-2597
AF12	001100	RFC-2597
AF13	001110	RFC-2597
AF21	010010	RFC-2597
AF22	010100	RFC-2597
AF23	010110	RFC-2597
AF31	011010	RFC-2597
AF32	011100	RFC-2597
AF33	011110	RFC-2597
AF41	100010	RFC-2597
AF42	100100	RFC-2597
AF43	100110	RFC-2597
EF PHB	101110	RFC-3246
VOICE-ADMIT	101100	RFC-5865

Fig 5.2

Flow Label

The 20-bit Flow Label is the only new field in the IP header.

All packets that are part of the same conversation are considered part of a "flow." Traditionally, flows are determined by using five identifiers in a packet. These would be the layer 3 source_address, destination_address, and protocol value, and the layer 4 source_port and destination_port.

As an example, if a host with an address of 2001:db8:1:1::3 is talking to another host with an address of 2001:db8:3:3::5 using the two communication methods, such as an http session and a telnet session, there would be two different flows:

1st flow - src=2001:db8:1:1::3, dst=2001:db8:3:3::5, prot=tcp, src_prt=2037, dst_prt=80
2nd flow - src=2001:db8:1:1::3, dst=2001:db8:3:3::5, prot=tcp, src_prt=2042, dst_prt=23

Fig 5.3

These two different flows are uniquely identified by the values of the source_port and the destination_port in the TCP header. To process this, you have to look all the way up into the TCP header to associate these packets.

The Flow Label, if used, breaks this down to basically needing only two fields to make the flow connection: the source_address and the flow_label.

All packets that are part of the same flow would be tagged with the same flow_label identifier by the source.

The IPv6 specification also allows you to possibly embed hash keys within the bits of the Flow Label field and to use the label for flow state information.

Payload Length

In IPv6, the base header is always 40 bytes and never changes size. Because of this, the Total Length field from IPv4 was replaced with the Payload Length field in IPv6. This 16-bit field identifies the size of all information following the Destination Address field of this IPv6 base header. This will include any extension headers that have been attached as well.

Next Header

The 8-bit Next Header field replaces the IPv4 Protocol field. It identifies what information follows this specific header.

If there are no IPv6 extension headers applied, it will identify the layer 4 protocol being transported, for example, TCP, UDP, or ICMP. If an extension header is attached, the Fragmentation header for example, it will be identified here.

Hop Limit

This 8-bit field is the same as the Time-to-Live field in IPv4; it was just renamed. It restricts the lifetime that a packet can spend traversing the network. Every router that receives a packet will decrement this value by 1 until it is decremented down to 0. The router that reduces this field value from 1 to 0 will discard the packet and send a control message to the sender notifying the sender that the packet has been discarded due to the hop limit being exceeded.

Source Address

This field identifies the 128-bit address of the sender of the packet. This can be used as part of the flow identification, as described under "Flow Label." It is also used for traffic identification for security access lists, as well as for telling the recipient of the packet whom to respond to.

Destination Address

This 128-bit field identifies whom the packet is destined for. This is also used for traffic and flow identification. It identifies the end of the base header for IPv6 as well. The total number of bytes following this field is what is placed in the Payload Length field.

Extension Headers

What if I need to fragment a packet? How will the receiver know how to reassemble the fragments back into the packet if there is no field to provide the fragment data?

This is where extension headers come in.

As I mentioned earlier, the base IPv6 header was streamlined for processing efficiency and to eliminate any fields that are not necessary (Checksum) or not commonly used (Fragmentation, Options, etc.). Now if you need to include fragment reassembly information, Type-Length-Value (TLV) options, etc., you can use extension headers. As the name implies, they extend the capabilities of the IPv6 header.

IPv6 was designed with this capability in mind. Evidence of this is the renaming of the IPv4 Protocol field to the IPv6 Next Header field. Protocol would imply a different protocol that is being transported, such as UDP, TCP, ICMP, or OSPF. Next Header may imply a new layer 4 header (UDP, TCP, etc.) but can also identify an extension header for IPv6.

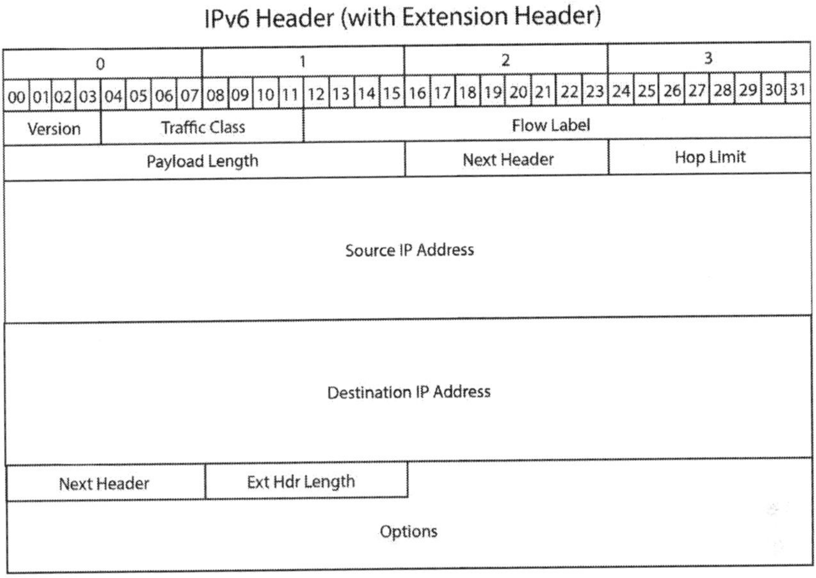

IPv6 Header (with Extension Header)

0	1	2	3
00 01 02 03 04 05 06 07	08 09 10 11 12 13 14 15	16 17 18 19 20 21 22 23	24 25 26 27 28 29 30 31

Version	Traffic Class	Flow Label	
Payload Length		Next Header	Hop Limit

Source IP Address

Destination IP Address

Next Header	Ext Hdr Length	

Options

Fig 5.4

The first field of every extension header is another Next Header field used to identify what follows this extension header. It could be another extension header, or it could simply identify the layer 4 protocol being transported. This behavior allows the simple "daisy-chaining" of additional extension headers as necessary to provide whatever capabilities are needed at layer 3 within IP.

When adding extension headers to IPv6, apply them in the following order (if used):

1. Hop-by-Hop Options header
2. Destination Options header (if you are using a Routing header and want each destination listed in the Routing header to process options)

3. Routing header

4. Fragmentation header

5. Authentication header

6. Encapsulating Security Payload header

7. Destination Options header (for options processed only by the ultimate destination)

Let's take a look at each of these.

Hop-by-Hop Options (NH = 0) and Destination Options (NH = 60) Headers

Hop-by-Hop Options / Destination Options

0								1								2								3							
00	01	02	03	04	05	06	07	08	09	10	11	12	13	14	15	16	17	18	19	20	21	22	23	24	25	26	27	28	29	30	31
Next Header								Ext Hdr Length								Option Type								Opt Data Length							
Options																															

Fig 5.5

We use two different headers to provide Type-Length-Value (TLV) options in the IPv6 header. The difference between each of them is in who processes the options being sent.

The Hop-by-Hop Options header, identified with a next header value of 0, will be processed by every router (hop) in the path between the sender and the destination.

The Destination Options header, identified with a Next Header value of 60, is processed by the destination host.

If the Destination Options header is used with a Routing header, each router in the predefined path will process the TLV Options in this header. If no Routing header is present, the TLV Options will be processed only by the final destination of the packet.

Routing Extension Header (NH = 43)

Routing Header

0								1								2								3							
00	01	02	03	04	05	06	07	08	09	10	11	12	13	14	15	16	17	18	19	20	21	22	23	24	25	26	27	28	29	30	31
Next Header								Ext Hdr Length								Routing Type								Segments Left							
Reserved																															
Address [1]																															
Address [2]																															

Fig 5.6

The Routing header, identified by the next header value of 43, was defined to support source-defined routing of the packets. You can do this only if the source knows what path to use for transporting the packets. An example of this would be to support mobility where you can define the path from the mobile devices' remote "care of address" to their stable "home address."

This header is not used much, especially because source routing is typically blocked through the service provider networks for security purposes.

Fragmentation Extension Header

Fragment Header

0		1		2		3		
00 01 02 03 04 05 06 07	08 09 10 11 12 13 14 15	16 17 18 19 20 21 22 23	24 25 26 27 28	29 30	31			
Next Header	Reserved	Fragment Offset			Res	M		
Identification								

Fig 5.7

In IPv6, the only device that can fragment a packet is the originating source of the packet. A Path Maximum Transmissible Unit (MTU) discovery process is performed, and if any link in the path has an MTU that is too small for the packet, the source will fragment the packet (see note) and apply the Fragment extension header to provide the reassembly information.

Note: The minimum supported MTU for IPv6 is 1280 bytes. If any link in the path between the source and the destination is less than 1280 bytes, the Path MTU discovery process will not work and the source will not know that it needs to fragment the packet. In this case, the IPv6 packet would have to be tunneled through another protocol, such as IPv4, and the fragmentation would have to be performed under the rules of the transporting protocol.

Authentication Extension Header (NH = 51)

Authentication Header

0	1	2	3
00 01 02 03 04 05 06 07	08 09 10 11 12 13 14 15	16 17 18 19 20 21 22 23	24 25 26 27 28 29 30 31
Next Header	Payload Length	Reserved	
Security Parameters Index (SPI)			
Sequence Number Field			
Authentication Data (variable)			

Fig 5.8

IPsec uses two different protocols to provide security protection to a traffic flow. One of these is the Authentication Header (AH), and the other is the Encapsulation Security Payload (ESP). Whenever an IPsec protection method is defined, it is provided by adding the proper extension header.

For example, if you are using OSPFv3 as your routing protocol and you configure OSPFv3 authentication for your IPv6 routing information updates, every OSPFv3 packet sent would include the AH extension header with the authentication information to validate the packet. Other, non-OSPFv3 traffic that has not been configured for IPsec will not include this extension header.

The AH header provides integrity checks to make sure that no bits have changed during the transmission. It ensures source authenticity so that you are sure that those you are communicating with are who they say they are. It also provides anti-replay protection.

AH does not provide any support for encryption and therefore no confidentiality of the communications.

Encapsulating Security Payload Header (NH = 50)

ESP Header

0								1								2								3							
00	01	02	03	04	05	06	07	08	09	10	11	12	13	14	15	16	17	18	19	20	21	22	23	24	25	26	27	28	29	30	31

Security Parameters Index (SPI)
Sequence Number Field
Payload Data (variable)
Padding (0 – 255 Bytes)
	Pad Length	Next Header
Authentication Data (variable)

Fig 5.9

The Encapsulating Security Payload (ESP) allows the transported data to be encrypted so it cannot be read by someone capturing the packets.

Encryption takes the clear text message being sent and processes it through an encryption algorithm, such as DES, 3DES, or AES, to convert it to an encrypted cypher-text that makes no sense to an eavesdropper. The recipient must be able to decrypt the cypher-text back into the clear-text message to read the contents.

Like the AH header, this extension header is applied only to traffic that has been configured for the IPsec-ESP protection, for example, OSPFv3 encryption instead of authentication.

Authentication, integrity, etc. is all included within the ESP protection for everything that follows this header. AH can provide protection for the information preceding the header as well.

When configuring IPsec tunnels, you identify how you want the traffic to be protected. You may use the AH header, the ESP header, or both. Most commonly, the ESP header is used with IPsec.

Now we know not only how the addresses work, but also how they are encapsulated when a communications packet is built by a network device. There is still more to IPv6, though. For example, how does a host learn the MAC address of a device it wants to talk to?

In the next chapter, we are going to move up the stack to layer 4 and see how IPv6 uses other protocols and control messages in order to function.

Chapter 6

Your Host Has Control Issues: Internet Control Message Protocol

Biggest ICMP myth: The utility PING was named after the phrase "Packet InterNet Groper."

"I Killed Your Packet"

Internet Control Message Protocol (ICMP) messages, as the name implies, are control messages sent between hosts to provide information about the network. Examples of these messages include things like "Are you there?" (ping–echo-request), "Yes I am here" (ping–echo-reply), or something like "Your hop limit is at zero so I killed your packet" (time exceeded). IPv6 uses these messages extensively in order to operate, much more so than IPv4 does.

Although ICMP is used to send control messages between hosts so they can operate correctly, over the years it has also been used for malicious purposes by hackers. Because of this, the common practice in IPv4 is to block all ICMP communications coming from outside the network. Blocking all ICMP cannot be done in IPv6 or it will stop operating. For example, a host would not be able to discover the destination MAC address that it needs for Ethernet encapsulation. Or the sender may generate packets that are too large to be passed through the end-to-end path.

All of the information that you need to send, transport, and receive a packet is provided within the IPv6 base and extension headers. However, IPv6 uses control messages that are transported at layer 4 to get all the information that is needed to properly build and control the communications.

In this chapter, we will look at how the Internet Control Message Protocol (ICMP) messaging is used by IPv6. We will also look at the five Neighbor Discovery messages and at how ICMP is used for Path MTU discovery.

What's above IP?

In IPv6, if there are no additional extension headers to apply, and identify, the Next Header field plays the same role as in IPv4 by simply identifying the next upper layer protocol being transported.

For the most part, these upper layer protocols are the same protocols being transported by IPv4. The Transmission Control Protocol (TCP) and User Datagram Protocol (UDP) have the same format and serve the same purpose as in IPv4. Other protocols, such as the Open Shortest Path First (OSPF) protocol, discussed with the routing protocols, have been updated to support specific features of IPv6.

ICMP for v6 is basically the same as it was for v4; however, additional message types are used to handle operational characteristics of IPv6. Let's take a look at of some of these now.

"Won't You Be My Neighbor?" —Mr. Rogers

So, what is a "neighbor"?

A neighbor is someone on your street (network segment) with whom you can share information directly. IPv6 groups neighbors in two categories: anyone who can speak IPv6, and routers.

IPv6 has an ICMP message type called Neighbor Discovery (ND). There are five types of ND messages:

> 133 – Router Solicitation
>
> 134 – Router Advertisement
>
> 135 – Neighbor Solicitation
>
> 136 – Neighbor Advertisement
>
> 137 – Redirect Message

Let's take a look at these based on their categorization.

Type 133 – Router Solicitation and Type 134 – Router Advertisement

When a host comes online, it immediately tries to learn about the network it is connected to. It does this by first sending out a type 133 ICMP message (Router Solicitation) to discover if there are any routers on its network segment. The destination address used for these Neighbor Discovery Router Solicitation (ND-RS) messages is FF02::2 (all routers multicast), and the source address is the sending host's link-local address (FE80:: . . .).

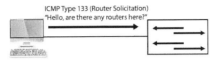

Fig 6.1

Any routers on the network segment, unless configured not to, will respond with a type 134 ICMP message (Router Advertisement) advertising their services as a "router." In this message, the routers will also provide all network prefixes assigned to this network segment.

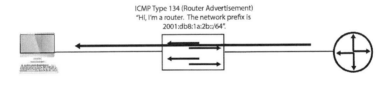

Fig 6.2

When the host receives this Router Advertisement (RA), it can determine the gateway router simply by looking at the source address of the RA. Using the network prefixes advertised in the RA message, the host can autoconfigure its own host address. (The interface_ID creation was discussed in chapter 4.)

Note: If the host already has an address on the advertised network prefix, manually configured for example, it will not autoconfigure a new host address.

Once the host has determined its address, it will use the

Neighbor Solicitation message to make sure no one else is using its address. This is the duplicate address detection (DAD) process.

Type 135 – Neighbor Discovery and Type 136 – Neighbor Advertisement

You cannot communicate with your neighbors if you do not have their physical addresses. Neighbor Discovery allows you to "discover" a neighbor that resides on the same network segment as you do. As part of this discovery, you also learn the MAC address of the neighbor.

In the following example, Host-A wants to talk to Host-B. Host-A knows Host-B's IPv6 address because it has been provided within the command (e.g., "Ping 2001:db8:f:e:234:56ff:fecb:a987") or, if a hostname was used (e.g., "Ping Host-B"), it was resolved by DNS. To create the layer 2 Ethernet encapsulation, you must be able to determine the physical layer 2 (MAC) address that you will use to communicate with Host-B.

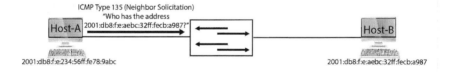

Fig 6.3

If both hosts are on the same network segment, as in figure 6.3, you will need to acquire the MAC address of Host-B directly. If the hosts are on different network segments, you will need to acquire the MAC address of your gateway router.

The host being solicited will respond with an advertisement message and provide its MAC address in the advertisement. When the requesting host receives this, it will add the advertising host to its IPv6 neighbor table along with the corresponding MAC address.

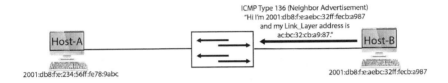

ICMP Type 136 (Neighbor Advertisement)
"Hi I'm 2001:db8:f:e:aebc:32ff:fecb:a987
and my Link_Layer address is
ac:bc:32:cb:a9:87."

Host-A

2001:db8:f:e:234:56ff:fe78:9abc

Host-B

2001:db8:f:e:aebc:32ff:fecb:a987

Fig 6.4

Okay then, if there are no broadcast addresses in IPv6, how does Host-A know whom to send the solicitation message to? Great question!

Host-A will convert the host IP address, which it knows, into a type of address called a solicited-node multicast address. Multicast addresses are, of course, designed to talk to two or more hosts at the same time. But this one is special because it is linked to the specific unicast IP address that Host-A is trying to communicate with and will, therefore, be received only by Host-B.

This layer 3 multicast address is determined so that you can discover the layer 2 address for that specific multicast group. This specific multicast address will be picked up only by Host-B and ignored by everyone else.

How is that address determined? You take the unique part of the IPv6 unicast address and append it to the standard multicast prefix for solicited-node multicast addresses. First, let's take a look at this address (I included the leading zeros for ease of reference):

2001:0db8:000f:000e:aebc:32ff:fecb:a987

Following our standard address allocation format, the first 32 bits (2001:0db8::) are the ISP prefix and would be the same for every customer that this service provider has assigned an address to. The next 16 bits (2001:0db8:000f::) would be the /48 site prefix assigned to the customer. Every address on this end user (EU) customer site would have these in common.

The next 16 bits are assigned the individual network, or "sub-network," from the organization's site prefix. So every host attached to this network segment will have this /64 bit prefix in common.

Good so far? Great. Now here's the fun part.

Of the 64-bit interface_ID, the first 24 bits make up the Organizationally Unique Identifier (OUI) of the host's MAC address, with the U/L bit flipped. (This OUI is ac:bc:32 without the U/L bit turned on.) This specific OUI is assigned to Apple, Inc. and would be the same for any Apple computer on this network segment that has a MAC address based on this OUI.

The next 16 bits (. . . ff:fe . . .) indicate that this is a EUI-64 derived interface_ID and would also be the same for every one of the previously mentioned Apple computers. So in this example, all of the Apple computers on this network segment would have the first 104 bits of their IP addresses in common

(2001:0db8:0001:0001:aebc:32ff:fe). That leaves just the remaining 24 bits to determine the uniqueness of this address (. . . cb:a987).

So out of the 128 bits in the address, only the least significant 24 bits are potentially unique.

The multicast prefix for solicited-node multicast addressing is FF02::1:ff00::/104 (see chapter 4). Keep in mind that you omit only leading zeros, not trailing zeros, when representing addresses. So the actual 104 bits for the prefix are "ff02::1:ff." You just take the least significant 24 bits of the IPv6 unicast address (cb:a987 in our example) and add them to the ff02::1:ff multicast prefix to get the layer 3 solicited-node multicast address for this host. In this example, it will be ff02::1:ffcb:a987.

The same rules apply for manually assigned addresses as well. For example:

Unicast –2001:db8:1:1::1 = Solicited-Node Multicast –ff02:1:ff00::1

Fig 6.5

Next, you convert this layer 3 multicast address into a layer 2 multicast MAC address to use as the destination for the Neighbor Solicitation message. You do this by taking the least significant 32 bits of the layer 3 multicast address (ffcb:a987 in our example) and appending it to the multicast MAC prefix of 33:33:. Once this is done, you get the destination MAC address of 33:33:ff:cb:a9:87 for the Neighbor Solicitation message for our example.

So in summary:

Unicast Address: 2001:db8:1:1:aebc:32ff:fecb:a987

Equals

Solicited-Node Multicast: ff02::1:ffcb:a987

Equals

Multicast MAC Address: 33:33:ff:cb:a9:87

What if you have two or more devices that have the same least significant bits? Won't they all receive the solicitation message and respond?

Yes, and no. First of all, each device's complete 48-bit MAC address must be unique, or you will have other communication problems. The OUI of the MAC address makes sure each vendor's addresses are unique.

Let's say you have a Hewlett Packard computer and an Apple computer on the same network segment and they both have MAC addresses ending in 4a:2f:f0. Each complete 48-bit MAC address will still be unique because of the assigned OUI. The Hewlett Packard has an OUI of 80:c1:6e, and therefore a 48-bit MAC address of 80:c1:6e:4a:2f:f0. The Apple has its OUI-based MAC address of ac:bc:32:4a:2f:f0, so the complete MAC addresses are unique.

EUI-64 uses the complete MAC address of the host when creating the interface_ID, so the layer 3 addresses will also be unique:

Unicast Addressing:
    HP –   MAC = 80:c1:6e:4a:2f:f0, IPv6 = 2001:db8:1:1:82c1:6eff:fe4a:2ff0
    Apple – MAC = ac:bc:32:4a:2f:f0, IPv6 = 2001:db8:1:1:aebc:32ff:fe4a:2ff0

Solicited-Node Multicast Addressing:
    HP –   MAC = 33:33:ff:4a:2f:f0, IPv6 = ff02::1:ff4a:2ff0
    Apple – MAC = 33:33:ff:4a:2f:f0, IPv6 = ff02::1:ff4a:2ff0

Fig 6.6

So, yes, because both hosts have the same least significant 24 bits of their addresses, they will both receive the same solicited-node multicast messages. But no, they will not both reply to the solicitation because the data in the payload of the Neighbor Solicitation message contains the exact IPv6 unicast address the solicitor is looking for. Only the host that exactly matches that address will send a Neighbor Advertisement message as a reply.

Because IPv6 is designed for hosts to be able to autoconfigure their addresses, the neighbor discovery process is also used for duplicate address detection (DAD). You can't have working communications when two or more hosts are using the same address. To avoid this, IPv6 nodes will send out Neighbor Solicitation messages for their own addresses to "detect" whether anyone else is using the same address.

If you send out a Neighbor Solicitation and receive a corresponding Neighbor Advertisement, the address is currently in use by someone else, so you cannot use it yourself. If you don't receive any replies, the address is available and you can use it.

Type 137 – Redirect

The fifth type of Neighbor Discovery ICMP message is the "Redirect" message. This is used if a host sends a packet to its default gateway and the best path is through another router on the same network segment. The default gateway router can send an ICMP Redirect message to the host telling it to send the packets to the other router on the network.

Path MTU Discovery

Because routers cannot fragment packets in IPv6, the source must be able to discover what the largest packet size, through the entire path, can be. You use ICMP messages to discover what the Path MTU size is for the upstream link.

When any router receives a packet that is too large to pass to an upstream link, the router will discard the packet and send a "Packet Too Big" ICMP message back to the source. The payload of the ICMP message will include the upstream MTU size that the source will have to conform to. The source will then fragment the message to fit within the upstream MTU size and retransmit it.

If there are multiple upstream links that have progressively smaller MTU sizes, this process will be repeated by each progressive router in the path. Once the source has the smallest MTU size for the end-to-end path, provided the MTU is equal to or greater than 1280 bytes, the rest of the packets for the flow will be fragmented as necessary to fit within the MTU of the path.

Whenever a packet becomes fragmented, you add the

Fragmentation extension header at layer 3. This extension header will contain the information necessary to properly reassemble the fragments back into the complete packet at the receiving end.

Find a Path

Now the hosts have all of the elements they need to be able to communicate with each other using IPv6. They have addresses, they have an encapsulation method, and they have a way to associate their neighbors' IPv6 addresses to MAC addresses for the Ethernet encapsulation. They even have a way to discover what the largest packet size they can transmit is.

What we need now is a way to find a path from the source to the destination and be able to forward the packets through the intermediate routers.

In the next chapter, we are going to look at how routers work. We will see the purpose of routing tables and how they are built. We will also look at some of the common routing protocols in use to build and maintain the routing tables.

Chapter 7

Get Your Kicks, on Route IPv6: Routing IPv6

> *Q: Which router bit is best for the binder channel of a dreadnaught?*
> *A: Wrong kind of router, and wrong kind of bit.*
> *(In case you didn't get that joke, I've been known to build guitars. Dreadnaught is a style of acoustic guitar.)*

Around the World in 380 Milliseconds

Routing is what makes the world go around. Well, at least it makes packets go around the world.

Okay, so you are migrating your network to IPv6. How are you going to get your new IPv6 packets from one end of the network to the other? Can you use the same routing protocols that you currently run for IPv4?

I have seen companies try to change their entire routing architecture to support IPv6 because they thought it would be more efficient. They added to the stress of the migration by also having to learn how a completely new, to them, protocol worked and was configured instead of sticking with what they already knew.

Routing protocol operations haven't changed between IPv4 and IPv6—but capabilities have changed. You don't need to learn anything big and new and scary, but you do need to be aware of the different versions and their compatibility with v4 and v6.

Why bother?

Not choosing the best protocol for your network probably won't kill you—but it can create a lot of additional stress. You may be trying to learn a new protocol just to support IPv6 when you don't really need to. Possibly, you could have poor paths selected or very slow reconvergence issues that cause you extra headaches.

Meanwhile, if you choose the right protocol for your needs, getting IPv6 up and running will be no more complicated than it needs to be. Choosing the right protocol will make everything easier and more effective. You could even save a lot of time and money not making a switch because you don't really need to.

So which protocol should you use? What are the choices, and when should you pick one over another?

Because this book is focused on the essential understanding of IPv6, we are not going to go into detail on configuring and deploying specific protocols. Instead, in this chapter we are going to take a look at how a router works in the world of IPv6 and the purpose of the routing tables. (No, these are not tables that hold your router, unless it's the other kind of router. Come on, get your head out of the woodshop.) We will then look at the commonly used routing protocols and why we may choose one over another.

What Is a Router?

So that you will better understand the use of routing protocols, it's probably best to start off with a basic overview of what a router does.

When you configure an end host (computer, printer, phone, etc.) for IP communications, you configure three things: IP address, a prefix length (subnet mask in IPv4), and a gateway. The gateway is the router, as discussed in the previous chapter in relation to Router Advertisement messages, that is used whenever the end host needs to talk to a host on a different network segment.

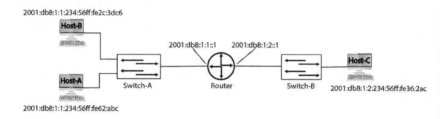

Fig 7.1

Take a look at figure 7.1. If Host-A wants to communicate with Host-B, Host-A will first check the destination address to see if it is on the same network segment as Host-A (a switch is a layer 2 device, so multiple ports can be on the same network segment).

In this case, they are both on the same network, so Host-A will check its IPv6 neighbor table to see if it already has the link-layer address (MAC address) of Host-B. If it does, Host-A will add the layer 2 encapsulation (Ethernet in this example) to the packet and send it out.

If Host-B is not currently in Host-A's neighbor table, Host-A will send out a Neighbor Solicitation to the solicited-node multicast address for Host-B (remember that from the last chapter?). When Host-A gets the Neighbor Advertisement message from Host-B, it will add Host-B to its neighbor table for future use.

Now, what if Host-A wants to talk to Host-C?

Host-C's address is on a different network segment (the first 64 bits do not match Host-A's address), so Host-A has to send the packet to its "gateway" router in order for it to be "routed" to the destination network.

Similar to the A-to-B communication, A will check to see if the MAC address of Host-C's router is in A's neighbor table and discover it by sending a Neighbor Solicitation if it's not. Host-A will then send the packet to the router with the router's MAC address as the destination of the Ethernet frame. Because the router is the destination for the frame, the router will pick it up and process it.

The router will check the layer 3 destination address in the IP header and see that the packet is not to the router itself. The router will then check its routing table to see if it has a path to the destination network and forward the packet appropriately.

The Routing Table

A router must have a path to the destination network of a packet to be able to forward it. If there is no path in the table, the router will discard the packet and send a "Destination Unreachable" ICMP message to the source.

You must have a way to populate the routing tables, of all the routers, with the appropriate information so they can reach any of the destinations in the network. The "appropriate" information could be the exact 128-bit destination host addresses, prefixes, summaries, or default routes.

Note: The "default route" is a destination address in the routing table set to all zeros, to imply all addresses. In IPv4, it is an all-zero address with an all-zero subnet mask (0.0.0.0 0.0.0.0). Likewise, in IPv6 it is an all-zero address with a prefix length of zero (0:0:0:0:0:0:0:0/0, or simply ::/0).

How do we get all of the destination prefixes, and routes, into the routing tables of each of the routers in the network?

That depends on how much work you want to do yourself, or if you're billing by the hour.

To start with, all address prefixes that are enabled on interfaces will automatically be added to the routing table. After all, you know how to get to network 2001:db8:1:1::/64 if you are directly connected to it. It will show up in the routing table as a directly connected route.

If you are not directly connected to a network, either the routes must be statically entered, or they can be learned dynamically from other routers by using a dynamic routing protocol.

Static routes are the most labor intensive because you must enter each one manually into the routing tables. Most commonly, static routes are used only for stub networks and default routes.

Dynamic routing protocols are most often used because they allow all the participating routers to exchange information to build and maintain their routing tables. This is also very useful for when changes occur to the network and the network needs to be reconverged so that each router can again find and use the best paths through the network.

The most commonly used dynamic protocols are RIP, OSPF, BGP, and EIGRP.

The Routing Information Protocol (RIP)

Common use: Labs and test environments

Hey, I thought "RIP" stood for "Rest in Peace." Yeah, well it probably should here as well, but some things just won't die.

Each of the IPv6 routing protocols is basically a variation of the IPv4 version of the protocol. They have been updated to support the IPv6 prefixes and to communicate over IPv6. Some, such as RIP, have been implemented as a new version of the protocol to operate with IPv6. Others, such as BGP, transport multiple address families (IPv4 and IPv6) within the same protocol process.

RIP is the great-grandfather of the IP routing protocols.

I won't bore you to death here with a discussion of all the differences between "distance vector" and "link state" protocols, but RIP is the distance vector protocol in the lineup. In basic terms, it cannot see past its adjacent neighbor routers, it has a very limited metric for determining the best path, it sends out full routing table updates every thirty seconds, and it cannot extend beyond fifteen hops (other routers) to reach any destination.

RIP version 1 was originally defined, for IPv4 addressing, in 1988 and contained a lot of limitations that restricted it from being a very useful protocol. It was updated to RIP version 2, to overcome many of the issues with version 1, in 1993, and it was last standardized in 1998. It was enhanced by using multicast addressing (224.0.0.9) for updates (version 1 used broadcast addressing) and supporting classless routing. Both version 1 and version 2 support only communication over IPv4 networks and updates for IPv4 prefixes.

RIPng (next generation) was introduced in 1997, as an update to RIPv2, to provide support for IPv6. RIPng operates the same as RIPv2 but allows the transport of IPv6 prefixes over IPv6 networks. Updates are sent out with the router's outgoing interface link-local (fe80:: . . .) address as the source and the RIPng multicast address (ff02::9) as the destination. RIPng communicates over the User Datagram Protocol (UDP) port 521.

RIP is very easy to implement but suitable only for very small networks. Its purpose is typically for quick lab setups where routing is necessary but not the point of the testing. Convergence is slow, and the metric, hop count, does not consider the bandwidth or any other link characteristics, so RIP is not well suited for any type of complex network design.

Open Shortest Path First (OSPF)

Common use: Small to large networks

In RIP, a distance vector protocol, a router cannot see beyond its directly adjacent neighbors and it has to trust that what the neighbors tell it is true. OSPF routers, in contrast, build their own view of the network from their own perspective by creating what is called a Shortest Path First (SPF) tree. Each router is the root of its own SPF tree. The routers then use that complete view of the network to determine the best, "shortest," path to any destination.

OSPF was introduced in 1989 as a routing protocol for large networks.

It was updated in 1991 to version 2. The update included adding a new area type called a "stub area." Stub areas allow for better implementation in larger networks by greatly reducing the number of routers involved in reconvergence updates whenever there is a change to the network topology. Version 2 also allows multiple Type of Service (ToS) entries to use the same routing table.

It was further updated again in 1994, also version 2, to fix an issue with virtual links and to add some minor enhancements such as the support for supernetting.

IPv6 support was added in OSPF version 3 in 1999 and further updated in 2008.

Although OSPF version 3 allows support for both IPv6 and IPv4, not all vendor implementations support IPv4 updates with it. If you are running one of these nonsupportive vendor implementations, and if you're running both IPv4 and IPv6 on the network, you will have to configure separate OSPF processes for each IP version. You will run OSPFv2 for the IPv4 addresses and OSPFv3 for the IPv6 addresses. If you have a supported vendor implementation, you can transport both IPv4 and IPv6 updates over OSPFv3.

OSPF is a link-state routing protocol. A link-state protocol does not share its entire routing table with its neighbors. Instead, an OSPF router shares only its "links" (interface connections to networks) that are currently active when it initially joins the network, and it advertises changes only when they occur, such as a new link coming up or an existing link shutting down.

To keep all the routers current, a simple hello message is periodically sent between neighboring routers to let each other know that they are still up and working. If a "hello" message is not received from a neighbor within the timeout period (called the "dead timer"), the neighbor is determined to no longer be available. At that point, the reconvergence process must take place.

OSPF is designed to work with a network architecture based on "areas." You may have one or more areas, but you must have a "backbone" area that is identified with the area ID of 0.

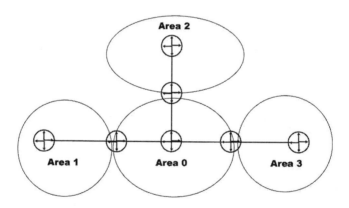

Fig 7.2

The area IDs are 32 bits in length, and you can represent them as either a decimal value or in a "dotted decimal" format, (like an IPv4 address). So your backbone area can be identified as either "Area 0" or as "Area 0.0.0.0"; both mean the same thing.

Every non-backbone area must have a connection directly to the backbone area for inter-area communications to occur. When a link-state advertisement (LSA) is received on a router's interface, it may be forwarded only to other interfaces within the same area in which the LSA was received, or it may be forwarded to interfaces in the backbone area.

If an area becomes segmented and no longer has a direct connection to the backbone, a "virtual link" to the backbone must be configured.

Each OSPF communicating interface on a router is assigned to a single OSPF area. This is used by the router to determine the specific types of communication packets to be sent and received through the interface. Most routers in a deployment will have all of their interfaces assigned within one area. These are simply called "internal routers."

Some routers support the inter-area communications and will have one or more interfaces assigned to Area 0 and other interfaces assigned to a different area. These routers are called "area border routers" (ABRs). This is where the support for large networks takes place. The ABR routers provide route filtering through route summarization to control what prefixes may be advertised between areas.

Assuming your subnet design is efficient, and contiguous subnet prefixes are contained within single areas, you can greatly reduce the number of prefixes being advertised throughout the network.

In figure 7.2, for example, you could have hundreds of network prefixes contained within "Area 1." Instead of advertising all of the prefixes to every router in the network, they could be sent to the other areas as a single summary prefix that would be advertised by the area border router from Area 1 to Area 0. That summary prefix could then be advertised into the other areas through each of their area border routers.

Any change that would occur, such as an interface going down or a new link coming up, would not affect the view of the network from the perspective of any routers in areas 0, 2, or 3, as long as the change was contained within the summary prefix. Therefore, none of the routers residing outside of the affected area (Area 1 in this case) would have to participate in any of the reconvergence updates. This allows support for networks scaling up to thousands of routers.

Border Gateway Protocol (BGP)

Common use: The internet

The Border Gateway Protocol (BGP) is the routing protocol used for the internet.

BGP was introduced in 1989 as an enhanced update to the Exterior Gateway Protocol (EGP) to support the virtually unlimited scalability of inter-domain routing.

It was updated in 1990 (version 2), again in 1991 (version 3), and then to the current version 4 in 1995. IPv6 support was added in 1999 through the use of multiprotocol extensions that allow the different address families to be advertised in the updates, including both IPv6 unicast and IPv6 multicast. The current update, still version 4, came in 2006.

RIP and OSPF are designed to work within an organization's

network. They are called interior gateway protocols (IGPs). BGP is designed to work between separate service provider and/or enterprise networks and is called an exterior gateway protocol (EGP). This is not meant to be confused with the predecessor to BGP, but . . .

Because BGP is the routing protocol for the entire internet, a lot of control must be implemented. A single change that you make, either accidentally or on purpose, can potentially affect the internet routing for the rest of the world.

Because of this, organizations that are peering with each other sign peering agreements. These agreements define the parameters of the peering relationship and the information that can be shared. Command access to BGP gateway routers is typically restricted to select personnel for this reason.

In BGP, each organization gets associated as a separate autonomous system (AS), and the assigned AS numbers are under the authority of the Internet Assigned Numbers Authority (IANA), just like the IP addresses.

Where in IGP protocols, such as RIP and OSPF, a "hop" is a transit through a router, in BGP a "hop" is a transit through another autonomous system. So a "path" in BGP may be (from Company-A to Company-C) Service Provider-1 – Service Provider-2 – Company-C ({AS}65001 {AS}65002 {AS}65030).

Once you reach the destination autonomous system (65030 in this example), the routing of the packet is handed off to the interior gateway protocol (IGP) within that autonomous system, such as OSPF.

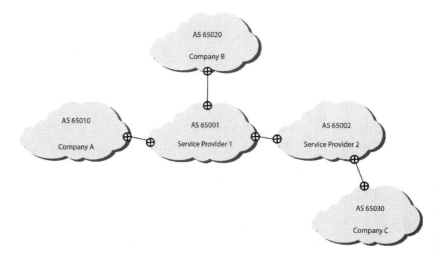

Fig 7.3

Other Protocols

RIP, OSPF, and BGP are standards-based, common routing protocols that are supported by all vendors. Two other protocols used for routing information updates are the Enhanced Interior Gateway Protocol (EIGRP) and the Intermediate System to Intermediate System (IS-IS) protocol.

Enhanced Interior Gateway Protocol (EIGRP)

Common use: Can be used only on Cisco routers

EIGRP is a routing protocol that is proprietary to Cisco Systems. As the name implies, it was developed as an enhancement to Cisco's Interior Gateway Routing Protocol (IGRP).

IGRP was initially created as a proprietary distance vector

protocol to overcome many of the limitations of RIP. IGRP reduced the frequency of routing updates from thirty seconds to ninety seconds, expanded the reachable distance from 15 hops to 254 hops, and utilizes a much better metric calculation instead of the basic hop count.

Where IGRP operated purely as a distance vector protocol, EIGRP enhanced the operations by also borrowing from the characteristics for link-state protocols. This includes using a keepalive message process instead of sending entire routing table updates periodically, using incremental updates to send out changes only when necessary, and being able to simulate the link-state area structures through interface-level summarization.

Because EIGRP is proprietary, it can currently be used only between Cisco routers. Cisco did announce, in 2013, intentions to release EIGRP to the public for use in multi-vendor environments, if other vendors choose to add it to their operating systems.

Intermediate System to Intermediate System (IS-IS)

Common use: Reclassified to "Historic" status in February 2014

The IS-IS protocol was created by the International Standards Organization (ISO) to work with the Open System Interconnection (OSI) protocol suite.

"Wait, I thought OSI was a model used to define the steps of communications."

It is, but ISO also created the OSI protocol suite to go with the model that was originally intended to replace the other protocol suites in use at the time such as TCP/IP, IPX, and AppleTalk.

In the OSI world, devices are classified as "end system" (ES) devices and "intermediate system" (IS) devices based on their location in a communication chain. An ES device would be your endpoint device, such as a computer or printer. An IS device is an "intermediate" device in the communication chain, such as a router. So the name "IS-IS" means it is used to share information between intermediate systems and other intermediate systems.

In the OSI protocol suite, the equivalent to the layer 3 Internet Protocol, or IP, is called Connectionless Network Service (CLNS). It has its own addressing structure that IS-IS was designed to support.

Because the thought at the time was that you would replace all the other protocol suites with OSI, IS-IS was designed to carry multiple address families, such as IP. This would make the transition to OSI much easier. As such, IS-IS can provide routing table update services for CLNS, IPv4, and IPv6 through the same protocol process, similar to BGP.

IS-IS is a link-state routing protocol, like OSPF, and was designed to support large scalable networks. Because the OSI protocols did not take over the world, and because most people are comfortable working with the other routing protocols such as OSPF, IS-IS was never deployed in many organizations. Several service providers had deployed it initially for the scalability aspects, but it never took hold in the enterprise market.

The Missing Piece

AWESOME! You now know all of the basic stuff about how IPv6 works. You understand the address format and how addresses are assigned. You know how the encapsulation works and what each field of the IPv6 header is used for. You know how IPv6 uses ICMP for things like acquiring addresses, associating a neighbor's IPv6 address to the MAC address, and Path MTU discovery. You even know what the routing protocols are and how routers use them to discover the network and properly forward packets to their destinations.

What if parts of your network are not able to transport IPv6? What if you have legacy hosts on your network that are not capable of communicating via IPv6?

In the next chapter, we will look at options for when you cannot exclusively run IPv6 on your network. We will discuss transition methods such as dual stacking devices and tunneling traffic across networks.

Chapter 8

Watch Out for the Worms: Transporting IPv6 in Mixed Environments

Worms? Isn't there a shot for that?
Not exactly, you just have to choose your tunnel wisely.

The Transition

I constantly have people tell me something like, "We have enough addresses to last us at least another fifty years; there's no need to migrate to IPv6."

My answer to that statement is usually something like, "Great, as long as you don't want to communicate with anyone outside of your company in the future, including customers, you are all set." I cannot answer the question of when IPv4 will cease to exist on the network, but I can tell you that all it will take is for a company that everyone wants to connect to, running only IPv6, to come along.

When the CEO of the company calls IT and asks, "Why can't I get to this website?" and you reply with something like,

"They have an IPv6 address and we are running only IPv4," what do you think will happen?

Until the world finally converts fully to IPv6, you will have to be communicating with, at least, IPv4 and IPv6 simultaneously as you migrate. So for now, yeah, you have to deal with this. Without a transition scheme in place, you could end up creating a "black hole" for some of your traffic. This could cause hosts, or entire network segments, to become unreachable.

Of course, until everyone is running IPv6, you will still need to be able to communicate with IPv4, or you will be unable to reach many places, including some email servers, web servers, and e-commerce sites.

So, you are going to set up IPv6 across your network. Life will eventually be so much easier.

The question now is will you still have any hosts or segments of your network that will be running only IPv4? Or are you going to be talking to anyone else that has only IPv4?

In either of those cases, you will have to support some type of transition mechanism. This could be tunneling IPv6 through part of the network, or dual stacking devices so they run both protocols simultaneously. You must decide which of these you're going to use any time you are going to have both protocols in operation, like during a migration.

In this chapter, we are going to discuss issues and techniques of handling IPv6 traffic during a transition. We are going to take a look at dual stack and tunneling approaches to support this.

Dual Stack

Dual stacking means you have both protocols running on the same computer at the same time. Let's check out the following host ifconfig example.

```
Richards-MacBook-Pro:~ richardkullmann$ ifconfig
lo0: flags=8049<UP,LOOPBACK,RUNNING,MULTICAST> mtu 16384
    options=3<RXCSUM,TXCSUM>
    inet6 ::1 prefixlen 128
    inet 127.0.0.1 netmask 0xff000000
    inet6 fe80::1%lo0 prefixlen 64 scopeid 0x1
    nd6 options=1<PERFORMNUD>

    {output omitted}

en0: flags=8863<UP,BROADCAST,SMART,RUNNING,SIMPLEX,MULTICAST> mtu 1500
    ether ac:bc:32:9f:c6:9f
    inet6 fe80::aebc:32ff:fe9f:c69f%en0 prefixlen 64 scopeid 0x4
    inet6 2001:db8:209:8700:aebc:32ff:fe9f:c69f prefixlen 64 autoconf
    inet6 2001:db8:209:8700:df1:fb35:4703:7be4 prefixlen 64 deprecated autoconf temporary
    inet 192.168.0.5 netmask 0xffffff00 broadcast 192.168.0.255
```

Fig 8.1

Figure 8.1 depicts a dual-stacked computer running both IPv4 and IPv6.

This is a capture of the interface configuration (ifconfig) command output on the computer I am writing this on right now. I did make some modifications to the output so that I am not giving out my actual global addresses (sorry, hackers), by changing my actual v6 prefix to a "2001:db8::" prefix (remember, 2001:db8::/32 is assigned for documentation purposes). I also modified my MAC address, and therefore my EUI-64 interface_ID.

In this example, the first interface is the "loopback" interface ("lo0"). It has both an IPv4 loopback address ("inet 127.0.0.1") and an IPv6 loopback address ("inet6 ::1") assigned to it. In addition, it also has a link-local address ("inet6 fe80::1 . . .") assigned on it. This is because, if you remember from earlier, every interface running IPv6 will have a link-local address. This includes the loopback interface as well because it is running IPv6.

The second interface shown (en0) also has both IPv4 and IPv6 running on it. The IPv4 address is "192.168.0.5" with a subnet mask of 255.255.255.0 ("0xffffff00"). This interface has three IPv6 addresses displayed: the link-local address of "fe80::aebc:32ff:fe9f:c69f," the autoconfigured EUI-64 global-unicast address "2001:db8:209:8700:aebc:32ff:fe9f:c69f," and the autoconfigured privacy address of "2001:db9:209:8700:df1:fb35:4703:7be4."

On both interfaces, following the link-local address there is a "%." What is that for?

Because the link-local address on every interface has the same prefix, fe80::, you cannot use the routing table to reach that network. You must have some other way of identifying what interface you will egress to reach a host on that specific fe80:: network. The "%" following the address identifies what interface to use.

The specific format of the interface ID following the "%" will vary depending on the system you are viewing. For example, in the MAC OSX (shown in figure 8.1) it is the interface name ("lo0" or "en0"). In Windows, it is displayed as the interface ID number ("4," "5," etc.).

To enable dual stacking, you just have to make sure that IPv6 is enabled on the host and then just assign both IPv4 and IPv6 on its interface(s). It's as simple as that.

This is the common initial step in migrating toward IPv6. It is easy to set up and allows access to hosts using IPv6 but still allows you to talk to IPv4 devices that have not been, or cannot be, migrated to IPv6. The infrastructure devices (routers, switches, firewalls, etc.) can be dual stacked to allow the transport of either protocol, and services can be dual stacked as they are added to the migration. We will look at this in the section on migration.

It's important to remember that in a dual-stacked environment you will basically have two different networks to maintain. Even though you are using the same equipment, cables, etc., you will have an IPv4 network and an IPv6 network. This means that everything you need to do to manage the IPv4 network, such as access lists, firewall rules, and routing protocols, will have to be duplicated for the IPv6 network. This can be very labor intensive, depending on the scope of your network, to initially implement.

You will also have to consider the system resources necessary to run this type of network. You need the device memory and processor resources to handle the multiple routing environments. Because the IPv6 address is four times the size of an IPv4 address, the memory required for routing tables, neighbor tables, and anything else that refers to an address will be much larger. Depending on the protocols being run, you also will have to duplicate neighbor tables, topology tables, etc.

Tunneling

When you have areas of the network that can run only one protocol, and you need to transit across them with another protocol, tunneling is your only option.

Tunneling is simply taking one protocol (IPv6 in this case) and encapsulating it within another protocol (IPv4) to transport it across the network.

You can set up the tunnels in several ways, but the end result is the same. In the case of figure 8.2, you have an IPv6 host communicating over an IPv4 network to talk to another IPv6 host.

The encapsulation process can be done on either an endpoint, such as a computer, or an intermediate device. In either case, whatever is doing the tunneling must be dual stacked so it can talk to both the IPv4 and the IPv6 networks.

The basic operation of this is the "IPv6IP" encapsulation (see figure 8.2), which takes the IPv6 packet (layer 3 ipv6 + payload) and encapsulates it as the payload for an IPv4 packet.

Fig 8.2

In this example, Host-A wants to talk to the web server Server-Z, both of which communicate via IPv6 only.

Host-A builds the packet for transport over IPv6 because that is all its network supports. Because the destination (Server-Z) has a different network prefix, Host-A will set the Ethernet destination as the default gateway (Router-A).

When Router-A receives the packet, it checks the routing table to figure out how to forward the packet toward Server-Z. In order for the packet to reach Server-Z, it will have to be sent across the IPv4-only network through Router-B to Router-C. Router-A will need to take the entire packet (IPv6 and above) and put it inside a new IPv4 packet. To do this, Router-A just creates a new IPv4 header and prepends it in front of the packet's existing IPv6 header. Router-A will make itself the IPv4 source of the packet, and it will make Router-C the IPv4 destination of the packet.

The payload will be identified in the IPv4 header's Protocol field as "41." This will tell Router-C that the payload following the IPv4 header is IPv6.

This new IPv4 packet, with the IPv6 payload, will be sent to the next-hop router (Router-B) and then forwarded to Router-C. When Router-C receives this packet and sees that it is the destination of the packet, it will process the IPv4 header. The protocol ID of 41 tells Router-C to pass the encapsulated payload to its IPv6 process. Now, it will be handled normally as an IPv6 packet.

Okay, that process is fairly easy, but how does Router-A know where to send the packet? This can be manually defined within the configuration, or it can possibly be automatically determined. Let's take a look at how that works.

6to4 Automatic Tunnel

Automatic tunneling requires some method of being able to automatically determine what the destination address of the tunnel is. 6to4 is one of those methods. It is not commonly used because of the specific addressing requirements, and when you cease to use the 6to4 tunneling, you will have to readdress your network.

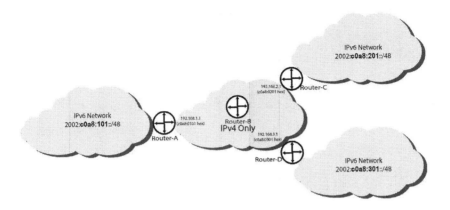

Fig 8.3

The 2002::/16 prefix is reserved for the use of 6to4 tunnels. Each IPv6 cloud participating in a 6to4 tunneled network is assigned a /48 prefix specific to the IPv4 address used to reach the cloud.

In figure 8.3, the IPv6 cloud attached to Router-A can be reached via Router-A's IPv4 address (192.168.1.1). To determine what that cloud's IPv6 prefix will be, you convert Router-A's IPv4 address into hexadecimal (c0a8:101) and prepend it with the 2002: 16-bit prefix (2002:c0a8:101::/48). You can then subnet this /48 prefix to the /64 prefix for each individual network within that cloud.

You do the same process for the IPv6 clouds attached to Router-C (2002:c0a8:201::/48) and Router-D (2002:c0a8:301::/48). A host in Router-A's IPv6 cloud that wants to reach a host in Router-C's cloud will forward the IPv6 packet to Router-A. Seeing that the destination address starts with "2002:", Router-A will use the 32 bits following the "2002:" to identify the destination for the IPv4 tunnel (c0a8:301 hex = 192.168.3.1 dec).

Did I mention that this is not commonly used? The problem with this type of implementation is that when full migration to IPv6 is accomplished, and you no longer need the tunnels, you will need to reassign all your addresses to your assigned global unicast prefix. This means that anything referring to an address, including DNS entries, firewall rules, and access lists, must also be reconfigured using the global addressing.

Intra-Site Automatic Tunnel Activation Protocol (ISATAP)

ISATAP is useful when your hosts are dual stacked but are connected to an IPv4-only network.

Like 6to4, ISATAP is also dependent on specific addressing, but it is much more flexible due to the addressing being within the least significant 64 bits of the address (the interface_ID). Because the tunnel destination is within the interface_ID, ISATAP will work with any prefix assignments. Each host automatically gets an associated ISATAP address for each IPv4 address enabled on the host.

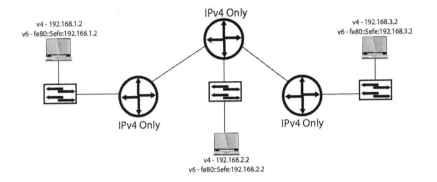

Fig 8.4

Every IPv4 address on a host gets prepended with the hex 5efe: and then appended to the network prefix, including the fe80:: link-local prefix. The encapsulation is still an IPv6IP encapsulation (protocol = 41), but the IPv4 tunnel endpoint is determined by the 32 bits following 5efe: (the least significant 32 bits).

Even though the name "Intra-Site" implies that this tunnel is within ("Intra") the network site, you can still communicate with IPv6 hosts that are external to your network by using a router attached to the external IPv6 network. Your internal host can use IPv4 to reach the external gateway router, and the packets can then be decapsulated and sent to the outside IPv6 network.

Teredo

What if you are using IPv4 NAT within your network? Then most of the tunneling methods will not work.

One of the big problems with the other tunneling methods that we have discussed is their use of the protocol identifier of

"41." If you have any infrastructure equipment that does not use IPv6 but does check the Protocol field, it typically will not know what to do with protocol 41.

A primary example of this is Network Address Translation (NAT) devices.

NAT uses the layer 4 source and destination ports, if known, as part of its translation table. This is what allows you to be able to have many internal hosts translating to the same external address, such as the outside interface address. In addition to translating the layer 3 IP addresses, each internal host will also get an associated port translation that will be added to the translation table.

If an IPv4 NAT device receives a packet with a protocol ID of 41, it can't identify source-port and destination-port fields and doesn't know what to do with the packet. This can also be an issue with IPv4 firewalls and router access lists.

So let's get to those worms.

The Teredo tunnel was designed to bypass these types of issues. It does this by creating a "bubble packet" that encloses the IPv6 traffic within a UDP transport and therefore hides IPv6 from the network.

The term "Teredo" is actually the name of a type of worm that burrows ("tunnels") through wood. This type of tunnel was basically designed for the purpose of penetrating your NAT device and other security implementations.

The original IPv6 packet becomes encapsulated with a new UDP header with the port ID of 3544. This new UDP traffic is then encapsulated within a new IPv4 header. Now, if a NAT device receives the IPv4 packet, the protocol ID is 17 (UDP), so NAT can use the UDP source and destination ports for its translations and forward the packet normally.

In order for Teredo tunneling to work, you need a Teredo server or relay attached to the IPv6 network to decapsulate and forward the traffic. This also requires using a specific addressing format. The 2001:0::/32 prefix is designated for Teredo addressing. The complete format for this address looks like this:

Prefix (32b) | Server_IPv4 (32b) | Flags (16b) | Port (16b) | Client_IPv4 (32b)
(2001:0000:)

Fig 8.5

The Teredo prefix is always 2001:0: to identify the type of address. The following 32 bits form the IPv4 address of the Teredo server. This is the endpoint IPv4 address for the tunnel. The following 16 bits are flags that identify the address type and NAT type. The next 16 bits are the mapped UDP port of the Teredo service. The final, least significant, 32 bits are the client's unique address.

Windows Vista and above have IPv6 enabled automatically and Teredo tunneling enabled.

The benefit of this is that you can communicate with remote IPv6 hosts from a Windows computer attached to an IPv4-only network. Because Teredo was basically created to circumvent security parameters, however, it has many potential security issues, so it is common practice to filter Teredo traffic on the network. Many government contracts require the filtering of Teredo traffic due to the potential security risks.

Full Communication

These are not meant to be permanent parts of your network. You should use these transition methods only where they are necessary to allow your full network communications while your systems are being migrated to IPv6. Once all of your hosts can communicate with IPv6, these techniques can be disabled.

At this point, we have covered all the essential information for understanding how IPv6 works, from the way addresses are represented to how they are assigned and how they get transported through the network, even if parts of the network do not support IPv6.

In the next chapter, we will take a look at things you should consider when planning a migration. Although there is no specific set of rules that define how a migration should occur, we will consider a possible strategy for migrating the network from IPv4 to IPv6.

Chapter 9

IPv4? We Don't Need No Stinking IPv4: Migrating to IPv6

> *In the slow race to deployment, what country was the first to reach 100 percent deployment of IPv6?*
>
> *The answer is Jersey. (It's a tiny country between England and France.)*

The Great Migration

If you're still using that archaic IPv4, now that you realize IPv6 is really cool you probably want to start migrating your network.

Now what do you do?

It is always best to have a strategy before you start an attack. (Kill IPv4!!) Without one you could, for example, have hosts that start trying to communicate over IPv6 before your network can transport it (creating a black hole). Worse, you could be creating new big openings in your network that attackers could exploit. Neither case is good.

Because every organization's network is different in its topology, the equipment being used, the services that are deployed, and so on, I can't give you precise step-by-step instructions that

113

will work in every environment. What I am going to show you here is the basic approach I typically take for migrating a network from IPv4 to IPv6.

The process goes like this:

1. Perform a site survey.
2. Upgrade, where necessary.
3. Dual stack the transport.
4. Build tunneling where necessary.
5. Dual stack the services.
6. Test the transport and access to services.
7. Add IPv6 services to DNS.
8. Dual stack the workstations.
9. Test and monitor.
10. Disable IPv4 where possible.

Let's look at each of these in turn.

Perform a Site Survey

First, make sure that all devices involved can work with IPv6.

You should start with a site survey, taking every device on the network into consideration. Does the operating system support IPv6? Do the services running on the host support IPv6? Do the applications, commercial and/or custom, work with IPv6? Anything that will not currently work with IPv6 will need to be upgraded, fixed, or replaced.

Even if a system supports IPv6, you may still want to consider whether it should be upgraded to work better.

For example, you may still have Windows XP computers on

the network (don't laugh; as of this writing, there are still a lot of them out there). Even though IPv6 is not enabled by default, Windows XP does support it. Windows XP is difficult to work with, however, because the IPv6 interface configuration cannot be performed within the graphical user interface (GUI). The interface configuration has to be performed from the command line using the "netsh" commands. Upgrading Windows will allow a much easier management of the host IPv6 parameters via the GUI, just like IPv4.

Then, do the services and applications on the network operate with IPv6?

For example, does an application use or reference IP addresses? Does it perform hostname to address lookups? If the use of a hostname is allowed, will it send out a DNS AAAA request to see if it can acquire an associated IPv6 address and use it?

Some applications may need to be upgraded by the vendor of the application, or an updated version may need to be installed. If you have custom applications that use IP addresses in the coding, the developers may need to recode the applications to work with IPv6. This can sometimes be an issue depending on the vendor.

With the site survey completed, not only will you have an updated inventory of what is on your network, but you will also have a good idea of what needs to be upgraded or replaced. With this information, you can plan the migration rollout. You may phase the rollout based on systems or applications that may need more time to be upgraded or prepared for the migration.

Upgrade Where Necessary

At this point, we still are not running IPv6 across the network. We are simply making sure that everything involved in this phase of the migration will be able to work when IPv6 is enabled. Armed with the site survey information, we can upgrade or refresh anything that currently does not support, or work with, IPv6.

As I said before, this does not apply only to devices without IPv6 support. It can easily apply to devices that currently do not have good support, as in the Windows XP example. Once we have everything running software that will work with IPv6, we can move on to the next step.

Dual Stack the Transport

Having IPv6 on your endpoint hosts and servers is useless if the packets between the hosts cannot be transported through your network. At this point, we can start making the infrastructure capable of forwarding IPv6 traffic.

This is where we will enable IPv6 on your routers, layer 3 switches, firewalls, IDS/IPS systems, etc.

If your IPv4 address scheme was well designed, you can typically convert your existing IPv4 subnets to hexadecimal and add them to your /48 site prefix. Because the binary values of the addresses will be the same, you can keep your existing route aggregation strategy and more easily duplicate your security configurations. If you do not have an efficient subnet scheme, now is a good time to correct it, as you assign your new IPv6 /64 prefixes.

Once we have the infrastructure equipment running IPv6, we can transport IPv6 traffic as well as the current IPv4 traffic. Verify that the network devices will be able to handle the load of managing the two logically different networks.

Now we start to examine and duplicate the security components of the network.

Every IPv4 access-list entry and every IPv4 firewall rule will need to be duplicated for IPv6, at least for the devices that currently will be running IPv6.

Build Tunneling Where Necessary

If for some reason you do not want to, or cannot, transport IPv6 through part of your network, but you still need IPv6 communications, tunnels may need to be created in order to provide the IPv6 transport over IPv4.

You may need to build tunnels internally in the network, externally through the service provider, or both. Keep in mind that the first phase here will be dual stacking. There are cases where a complete IPv6 network is built with no IPv4 support, but here we are looking at a simplified, and much less costly, approach.

As we discussed in the previous chapter, tunnels should be only a temporary solution and should not be considered as part of a permanent design. Tunneling has many potential issues, such as increased latency from the encapsulation/decapsulation processing, single point of failure issues, Maximum Transmissible Unit (MTU) size issues, and even issues that can occur with things like fragmentation.

If you are going to have isolated IPv6 islands in your network, tunneling will be necessary to communicate IPv6 between the islands. Or if your WAN service provider does not provide IPv6 transport, tunnels will be required between your network sites.

The point of dual stacking is to make sure that IPv4 communication will still work if some hosts, or part of your network, cannot communicate over IPv6. If the core of your network is dual stacked, tunnels are not necessary.

If you need tunnels for any reason, though, this would be a good time to implement them.

Dual Stack the Services

Now that you have the transport ready, and you have security elements in place, we can take a look at your servers. This is the point where you can dual stack your servers, such as your web servers and FTP servers.

DO NOT add these to DNS yet. Doing so could potentially black hole elements in your network. You don't even need to dual stack the DNS host server yet if you do not want to. That can be done later.

Test the Transport and Access to the Services

Now you need to test the connectivity of your network by communicating with the servers using their configured IPv6 addresses.

Can you reach it if you're supposed to? Is it being blocked if you're not supposed to be able to reach it? Check packet round-trip timers to verify the latency.

We want to make sure everything works as expected, excluding DNS, at this point. Test everything—around the network, internally on different subnets, across the WAN links, from outside the network, from wired connections, wireless access, and across the VPN.

Any issues during this testing can be addressed before the workstations start using IPv6. Once the workstation is dual stacked and DNS resolution works, the host will try to talk via IPv6 if it gets an address. By default, the use of IPv6 is prioritized over IPv4 because that is the migration path, from IPv4 to IPv6.

If there are any issues transporting the IPv6 traffic to the destination in the network, a black hole may exist and the workstation may not be able to reach to the server. In this step, we want to locate and address any of these issues before somebody "important" cannot get his or her email.

Add IPv6 Services to DNS

Now that we know the network is operating correctly and is secure, we can add the AAAA records to DNS for the services that should be reachable by name.

DNS is an application and may be accessed over either IPv4 or IPv6. It doesn't matter at this point if the DNS host computer is dual stacked or not, unless you are going to have any computers that are running only IPv6. Then they will have to be able to communicate with the DNS server through IPv6. Likewise, you must have IPv4 enabled on the DNS server as long as you have at least one computer communicating with it via IPv4 only.

In the past, it was a common practice to use a different fully qualified domain name (FQDN) for the IPv6 AAAA record than for the IPv4 A record. An example of this would be "www.hostname.com" for IPv4 and "ipv6.hostname.com" for IPv6. That is no longer the case.

The reason for using a different FQDN was so that a host that was not connected to an IPv6 network would not get black holed if it received an AAAA record response with an IPv6 address. Desktop operating systems should not issue an AAAA record request unless they have a valid global unicast address, so using different FQDN names should no longer be necessary.

We can also test the implementation now by trying to access each of the services by its hostname instead of typing in its IPv6 address. The hostname should be resolved to its address by DNS, and communications should work as expected.

Dual Stack the Workstations

Congratulations! You should now have a working IPv6 network.

The next step is to use it.

Keep in mind that unless you specifically disabled IPv6 on your workstations, this step may already be operational. If your desktop OS already had IPv6 enabled (you didn't disable it), it acquired an address as soon as you enabled its gateway router interface. Remember stateless autoconfiguration?

If this is not the case, you can now enable IPv6 on your

endpoint devices. Once IPv6 is operational, the devices will be able to acquire an IPv6 address and start using the network. You can also manually configure the addresses if you want.

If the host is dual stacked and a communication request is made, web-server access for example, the host will send out both a DNS A record request for an IPv4 address and an AAAA record for an IPv6 address.

If the destination server is not configured for IPv6 communication, only an A record response will be received. The host will use the IPv4 address received to communicate with the server. If the host does receive an AAAA record response, the host will use IPv6 to communicate with the server.

Test and Monitor

As someone reading this book, you are probably already aware that you cannot just set it and forget it. Things change, new bugs are found in software, traffic patterns change because links fail or new links are added, and even the increased load from dual stacking the network can create issues that you didn't previously find or expect.

To quote an old military phrase, "Improvise, adapt, and overcome."

You always need to stay on top of what is happening in your network so you can stay ahead of any issues, especially in current times, when people depend heavily on their networks. So don't just set it, forget it, and hit the beach, although that would be really nice right now.

Ahhh, I can feel the warm sand surrounding my toes as

I savor that first sip of my margarita. Oh wait, where was I? Oh yeah, back to IPv6.

Disable IPv4 Where Possible

If you monitor the traffic that is traversing your network, once everything is capable of operating over IPv6, you should notice that the only IPv4 traffic left on the network should eventually just be control traffic. All of the data communications should be operating over IPv6.

At this point, you can begin disabling IPv4 on the network.

You may still have some hosts that are not able to communicate with IPv6, so you will have to keep IPv4 in the infrastructure as long as those legacy hosts are still deployed. For this purpose, you should start any disabling of IPv4 from the edge of your network. The transport portion of your network should continue supporting IPv4 until you are sure it is no longer needed.

Now you not only understand how IPv6 works but also have a strategy for implementing it on your network. You understand pretty much everything about it: how the address is represented, its encapsulation methods, its routing operations, and how to forward it across a non-v6 network.

Where do you go from here?

Now that we have covered all the basics, the last chapter will take a look at what to do next.

Chapter 10

Well, That Was Fun: Where Do We Go from Here?

> *"The best way of learning about anything is by doing."* — *Richard Branson (A cool first name)*

What's the Rush?

Question: From the time we started tracking the types of traffic on the internet, what was the largest bandwidth load?

Answer: Porn

What changed this statistic? "Social media," specifically MySpace at the time. As of 2017, the largest load is Netflix.

Many "experts" I meet see the entire world only from their network's perspective. One of the top comments I hear about IPv6 is that there is no rush. "We have plenty of IPv4 addresses to last a long time."

What they don't realize is that we are out of IPv4 addresses as a whole, from the registry perspective. All it will take is a new company like Facebook or Netflix that can get only an IPv6 address to cause a rapid forced migration to IPv6 across the world.

The question is, when (not if) it happens, will you be ready?

What Next?

Now that you have an understanding of what IPv6 is and how it works, the next step is to start setting it up.

This is where the differences come in. Are you deploying it on Windows (pre-Vista or post-Vista?), Mac OSX, or Linux? What vendor routers are you using? What about layer 3 switches, firewalls, intrusion prevention system devices, or load balancers? These are just a few considerations.

This book aimed to build an essential understanding. We did not get into specific configuration commands because they will differ depending on what vendors and operating systems you are using. If I tried to include all the configurations, this book would easily be more than one thousand pages and wouldn't be nearly as fun.

You can contact your vendors for implementation-specific help or check the documentation for their products. Keep in mind that the implementation may even vary between different products from the same vendor. For example, the configuration in Cisco's IOS is different from Cisco's IOS-XR. All of this needs to be considered as well.

You can contact me as well if you need additional support. My team and I have experience in all realms, from working with small local telco service providers to assisting multinational organizations. We can help with subject matter expert guidance all the way to handling the full deployment or migration.

You can also attend, or host, one of my in-person training sessions on IPv6. Contact information is provided at the end of the book.

If you want to get connected via IPv6 and play around with it, without having to do a network migration, there are a couple of tunnel broker services that you can use. One is Hurricane Electric, at https://tunnelbroker.net/, and the other is SixXS (Six Access), at https://www.sixxs.net/main/. Both of these provide free connectivity services to communicate with IPv6.

September 24, 2015. That is the date on which ARIN depleted its IPv4 address pool. People haven't stopped connecting to the internet, and companies haven't stopped making devices that use addresses. Do you want to be someone who waits until the last minute to try to make it work during an emergency, or do you want to get ahead of the curve and ensure smooth sailing for yourself as others rush around madly?

Ready to Rock

By this point, I hope that you are much more comfortable with IPv6 and realize it doesn't suck as badly as you thought it did when you started reading this book. Even though the address, from the outside, looks much more complex and scary, it is really much easier to work with. Now that you understand it, you can see that there is only a digit or two that you need to focus on for most situations.

Hopefully, we have eliminated any doubts you had about working with IPv6 and you feel more confident in discussing it.

Whatever your reason for reading this book, whether you are starting a deployment, are preparing for a certification exam, or maybe just wanted to know more about IPv6, send me an email to let me know how it went. I'd love to hear from you.

Though this protocol has been pushed away and avoided for more than two decades, it no longer can be ignored if you want to progress technologically. Go out, kick some old protocol ass, and make some money, because you are one of the few who understand IPv6.

Now, where is that beach and cocktail?

ABOUT THE AUTHOR

Richard Kullmann is the founder of T6 Solutions, a consulting firm that advises service providers, global enterprises, and government entities on networking and security solutions. A sought-after consultant and educator with an international reputation, Kullmann has trained tens of thousands of people on networking technologies worldwide.

Kullmann has advised on the migration to IPv6 at numerous Fortune 500 companies. He is a Certified Novell Instructor, Microsoft Certified Trainer, Cisco Certified Systems Instructor, and Ciena Carrier Ethernet and Optical Communications Instructor.

Kullmann is a member of the Flying Samaritans, a volunteer organization that operates free medical clinics in Baja California, Mexico. When not in a hotel (or tent) somewhere in the world, he resides in Phoenix, Arizona.

Are you ready for IPv6?

T6 Solutions has resources to help you fully understand and deploy IPv6 within your organization. Learn to:

- Fully understand the parts and format of an IPv6 address
- Deploy IPv6 addresses efficiently
- Understand how IPv6, as a protocol, behaves on your network
- Efficiently route IPv6
- Migrate your specific network to IPv6

T6 Solutions offers webinars, workshops, and one-on-one consulting to help you and your team make sense of your unique situation, so you can leave the frustration behind and join the future.

To learn more, contact Richard at rkullmann@t6solutions.com, or follow him on LinkedIn: https://www.linkedin.com/in/richardkullmann

Made in the USA
San Bernardino, CA
16 June 2017